Acknowledgments

Writer
Dave Privett

Recording Studio
Ritz Studio Productions

Founder
Dr. Henrietta Mears

Publisher
William T. Greig

Managing Editor
Karen Stefacek

Project Editor
Tim Carpenter

Editor
Bob Rubinow

Art Director
Rachel Campbell

Scriptures quoted from the Contemporary English Version, © 1995, American Bible Society, New York, NY 10023. Used by permission.
Scriptures quoted from the New King James Version, © 1979, 1980, 1982, 1997, Thomas Nelson, Inc., Nashville, TN 37214. Used by permission.

All rights reserved. No part of this book may be reproduced in any manner whatsoever without written permission from the publisher, except where noted. For information, write to the attention of the Copyrights/Permissions Assistant.

Originally published by Strang Communications in 2004.

© 2006 Gospel Light, Ventura CA 93006. All rights reserved. Printed in the U.S.A.

Gospel Light

Acting God's Wo[rd]

32 skits that will giv[e] ministry to children. Each script is available on an enhanced CD as bo[th] a prerecorded audio script and as a written script that can be customized to suit your personal preferences.

By including more involved staging and use of props, these skits can also be used with a live drama team. With minor adaptations, all 32 scripts are interchangeable for use with puppets and as live dramas.

Here's How to Use *Acting God's Word:*

Each skit has been written with a related Bible passage in mind. After the title of each skit, you will find the correlating scripture passage and description. For example: Genesis 1:26–31 God Creates People

The purpose of this is to help your kids better understand the Bible passage and how to apply the message to their own lives.

You know your kids best—make the application of this creative material personal and relevant to your group.

Each skit begins with:

The Focus
The specific biblical point you want to minister to the kids

The Characters
The names and descriptions of the characters

The Props
Items to gather and prepare to add to the drama

The Setup
Practical ideas of how to prepare the props and staging, as well as a description of the setting in which the skit or drama takes place

Note: These puppet and drama skits were created to add a visual component to the Bible lessons included in *The Next Generation—KIDS Church 2*. To learn more about this full year of children's church curriculum, which takes kids on an adventure from Genesis to Revelation, contact your sales consultant at (800) 4-GOSPEL or go to www.gospellight.com.

Table of Contents

Unit 1 — Beginnings

Detective Doodad and the Case of the New Neighbor. 5
    LESSON 2   *Genesis 1:26–31*   *God Creates People*

Detective Doodad and the Strange Package. 8
    LESSON 3   *Genesis 3:1–24*   *The Fall of Man*

Detective Doodad and the Mysterious Message. 11
    LESSON 5   *Genesis 17:1–10, 15–22*   *Abraham and Sarah Have a Child*

Climb Every Mountain. 14
    LESSON 6   *Genesis 22:1–19*   *Abraham and Isaac at the Altar of Sacrifice*

The Doodad Gang and the Case of the Perilous Park Patron. 17
    LESSON 8   *Genesis 37*   *The Story of Joseph*

Unit 2 — On the Road Again!

The Doodad Gang Spreads the News. 20
    LESSON 9   *Exodus 3:1–22*   *The Call of Moses*

Special Delivery. 23
    LESSON 10   *Exodus 12:1–13*   *The Story of Passover*

Detective Doodad vs. the Decepto-Bots. 26
    LESSON 12   *Numbers 13:17–14:1*   *The Report of the Twelve*

Detective Doodad and the Dangerous Devices Department. 28
    LESSON 13   *Joshua 3:1–17*   *Joshua Leads Into the Promised Land*

Unit 3 — God's Mighty Heroes

Faith Factor. 31
    LESSON 14   *Judges 6:11–18*   *The Story of Gideon*

The Doodad Gang and the Capture of the Conniving Doctor. 34
    LESSON 17   *1 Samuel 17:32–50*   *David and Goliath*

Wise or Not So Wise. 37
    LESSON 18   *1 Kings 3:5–15*   *Solomon Asks for Wisdom*

Detective Doodad and the Caged Convincer. 40
    LESSON 19   *1 Kings 18:20–39*   *Elijah and the Prophets of Baal*

Watch Out World, I'm Packing Praise. 43
    LESSON 21   *2 Chronicles 20:2–26*   *Jehoshaphat's Great Victory*

Detective Doodad and the Hostile Hearing. 46
    LESSON 22   *Esther 2:17; 4:14*   *Esther Saves Her People*

Unit 4 — God's Word in My Heart

What Were We Made to Do?. 49
    LESSON 23   *Psalm 63:1–8*   *Seeking God's Face in Worship*

The Doodad Gang on the Hunt..51
    LESSON 25   *Isaiah 6:1–8*   *Isaiah's Call*

Detective Doodad and the Opulent Offer..54
    LESSON 26   *Ezekiel 37:1–14*   *Ezekiel and the Dry Bones*

The Town Where Everybody Rides..57
    LESSON 29   *Habakkuk 2:2–4*   *The Vision of Habakkuk*

The Doodad Gang and the Powerful Presence..59
    LESSON 30   *Haggai 1:2–2:9*   *Haggai and the New Temple*

▶ Unit 5   God in Sandals

Detective Doodad and the Anti-Attitude Attack..62
    LESSON 32   *Matthew 5:1–12*   *The Beatitudes*

The Ultimate Calling Plan...65
    LESSON 33   *Matthew 6:9–15*   *The Lord's Prayer*

Sick Survivor...68
    LESSON 35   *Luke 5:17–26*   *Jesus Heals a Lame Man*

The Doodad Gang and the Case of the Cut Off Connection..............................71
    LESSON 36   *Luke 15:11–32*   *The Story of the Prodigal*

Dr. D. Seaver Dupes the Doodad Gang...74
    LESSON 37   *John 13:1–5, 12–17*   *Jesus Washes the Disciples' Feet*

▶ Unit 6   Church Outside the Walls

Power Stan Finds His Voice..77
    LESSON 39   *Acts 2:1–18*   *The Early Christians Preach the Gospel*

Detective Doodad and the Missing Member...80
    LESSON 40   *Acts 3:1–20*   *The Miracle at the Gate*

The Doodad Gang and the Place of Persecution..83
    LESSON 41   *Acts 6:8–15; 7:54-60*   *Stephen's Persecution*

▶ Unit 7   Paul's Pen Pals

The Spirit's Most Wanted..86
    LESSON 45   *Galatians 5:22–23*   *The Fruit of the Spirit*

Detective Doodad Sticks to It and Gets His Man......................................88
    LESSON 47   *Philippians 4:10–20*   *The Unlimited Potential in Every Christian*

▶ Unit 8   The Last Word

Dr. D. Seaver Gets What He Asks For...91
    LESSON 50   *James 3:1–10*   *The Power of the Tongue*

He Gave Me the Gifts That I Give..94
    LESSON 51   *1 Peter 4:7–11*   *Using Your God-Given Gifts*

ADDITIONAL RESOURCES..45, 61

Characterization

Twenty puppet skits include the following characters:

Detective Doodad: a brilliant yet eccentric detective who is seen as "cool" in the eyes of his team of kid helpers. He has his wacky side and isn't perfect, but he always seems to come up with the right answer in sometimes unexpected ways. The kids respect him and know his true genius, but they occasionally forget that the great Detective Doodad knows exactly what he is doing. Dressed in a fedora hat and navy suit, Detective Doodad solves cases with the help of a handy jetpack, a laser-light that can see through walls, his wrist-communicator and more.

Tony: a natural leader who tends to jump in with both feet. He is smart, enjoys attention and is continually calling the other kids to action. He likes to analyze everything and is often two steps ahead of the group.

Keona: a sensible and intelligent girl who likes to work things out. She is truly the brains of the whole operation. Polite, but not always quiet, Keona steps up to the plate when needed. She is a level-headed thinker and is able to be independent of the other kids.

Henry: a good listener who comes across as tough, but is gentle. Give him a computer, and he'll find your answer in no time! He is loyal to the cause and especially to Detective Doodad.

New this year:

Mindi Lee: the newest member of the group. She is seemingly shy and hangs around with Keona. Don't be fooled by Mindi Lee's quietness, because when she needs to, she will fight for what is right. Her Asian customs are important to her, and she teaches the kids to be sensitive to other cultures.

Dr. D. Seaver: Detective Doodad's childhood friend and present-day archenemy. He is a master of disguise, so he may show up as himself or as a teacher, coach or neighbor who attempts to deceive the Doodad Gang into believing a lie. He takes the Power Point, or main message of the skit, and twists it. He tries to get the gang to question Detective Doodad's integrity, but in the end, he never wins.

Twelve puppet skits include a wide variety of different characters.
See each script for descriptions and characterization.

LESSON 2

Detective Doodad and the Case of the New Neighbor

Genesis 1:26-31   God Creates People

Focus: God has designed each of us to be special. We should accept and love other people no matter how different they seem. Kids need to know that they are designed by God.

Characters:

Detective Doodad: a brilliant yet eccentric detective who somehow always has the right answer.
Tony: a natural leader who tends to jump in with both feet.
Keona: a sensible and intelligent girl who likes to work things out.
Henry: a younger boy who looks tough, but is gentle. Give him a computer, and he'll find your answer in no time.
Mindi Lee: the new girl in town. She's seemingly shy, but not afraid to fight for what's right.

Props: Cardboard box with Chinese letters on it.

The Setup: The Doodad Gang clubhouse, then outside Mindi Lee's house.

[Begin music.]

Announcer: *[Offstage]* Time now for an exciting adventure with Detective Doodad and the Doodad Gang! The brilliant Detective Doodad, along with his team of helpers, Tony, Keona and Henry, are out to shine the light of truth upon the dark streets of Techno City. Today we find the Doodad Gang debugging their Communicators. Little do they know, a new mystery lurks just around the corner.

[Music fades. Detective Doodad, Tony and Keona enter.]

Detective Doodad: *[Working with communicator]* There! Try it now, Tony.

Tony: *[Speaks into wrist]* Tony to Keona. Come in, Keona.

Keona: I hear you loud and clear.

Tony: You fixed it, Detective. You're the best!

Detective Doodad: I just had to adjust the frequency. You shouldn't have any more problems with garage door openers.

Tony: I hope not.

Keona: Tony couldn't walk to school without opening every garage door on the block!

[Henry bursts into the room.]

Henry: Spies! Spies! *[Gasping]* Spies have kidnapped my neighbors!

Detective Doodad: Slow down, Henry. What seems to be the problem?

Henry: It started a few days ago, Detective. We didn't see our neighbors, the Andersons, all week. Yesterday, this weird-looking family showed up and started living in their house.

Tony: They must be holding the Andersons for ransom!

Detective Doodad: A good detective never jumps to conclusions. We need more facts before we'll know the truth.

Keona: What makes you think they're spies, Henry?

Henry: They talk funny, and they have lots of strange-looking stuff.

Tony: Let's call the feds!

Detective Doodad: Hold on a minute, Tony. We're going to examine the clues before we make up our minds. Put on your thinking caps, everyone. The Doodad Gang is on the case!

[Everyone exits. Transition music plays as the setting shifts to Henry's *neighborhood.* Tony *and* Keona *enter.]*

Tony: We've been searching for 20 minutes, Keona, and haven't found a thing. Let's call the cops.

Keona: Detective Doodad said not to do anything until we had all the facts.

Tony: *[Looking down]* Keona! Look at this box. *[Tony sets a box on stage with Chinese letters on it.]* Look at the strange writing! It must be some kind of unbreakable code. I knew these people were spies.

[Detective Doodad and Henry enter.]

Detective Doodad: What's this, you two?

Keona: Tony thinks he found a box with a secret code.

Henry: They have lots of boxes with that writing on it. They must be spies!

Tony: Yeah, let's call the National Guard!

Detective Doodad: Go, go, Doodad Magnifying Glass. *[Doodad examines the box.]* Hmm, it's just as I suspected.

Henry: Is it a secret code?

Detective Doodad: No, it's Chinese.

Tony: Chinese? We'd better call the CIA!

Keona: Chinese isn't a code, Tony—it's a language. Millions of people speak Chinese every day. This box could say "Rubber Ducky" on it for all we know.

Mindi Lee: *[Enters]* Actually, it says "Handle With Care."

Tony and Henry: *[Scream]* Aaaah! A spy!

Mindi Lee: Spy? I'm not a spy. You're the ones sneaking around people's houses.

Detective Doodad: Please forgive us for intruding, Miss Uuhh?

Mindi Lee: Hi. *[Shyly]* I'm Mindi Lee. My family just moved here from Hong Kong.

Henry: If you're not a spy, then what are you?

Keona: She's your new neighbor, Henry.

Tony: But why do you look so different from us?

Mindi Lee: Because that's how God made me. Besides, most of the kids where I come from look a lot like me.

Detective Doodad: Mindi Lee is from a different culture, Tony. People don't look the same all over the world. God made us in many different sizes, shapes and colors. That's why each of us is special.

Keona: I'm glad God made us special. The world would be pretty boring if we all looked the same.

Henry: Mindi Lee, I'm sorry for thinking you were a spy.

Mindi Lee: It's OK, Henry. I thought you were my cat. You guys make a lot of noise.

Henry: Hey Detective Doodad, could Mindi Lee join the Doodad Gang?

Detective Doodad: It'd be an honor to have her on our team, Henry.

Mindi Lee: What's a Doodad Gang?

Henry: Don't worry, Mindi Lee, we'll tell you all about it!

[All exit. Begin music.]

Announcer: *[Offstage]* As the sun sets, a new chapter begins for the expanded Doodad Gang. With the addition of Mindi Lee, what new challenges await them? Stay tuned for the continuing adventures of Detective Doodad and the Doodad Gang!

[Fade music.]

LESSON 3

Detective Doodad and the Strange Package

Genesis 3:1–24

The Fall of Man

Focus: Deciding to do wrong when you know what's right keeps you from God and all the good plans He has for you. Disobedience is dangerous, because sin separates you from God.

Characters:

Detective Doodad: a brilliant yet eccentric detective who somehow always has the right answer.
Tony: a natural leader who tends to jump in with both feet.
Keona: a sensible and intelligent girl who likes to work things out.
Henry: a younger boy who looks tough, but is gentle. Give him a computer, and he'll find your answer in no time.
Mindi Lee: the new girl in town. She's seemingly shy, but not afraid to fight for what's right.
Dr. D. Seaver: Detective Doodad's childhood friend and present-day archenemy, a master of disguise.

Props: Cardboard box or wrapped package.

The Setup: The Doodad Gang clubhouse.

[Begin music.]

Announcer: *[Offstage]* Boys and girls, it's time once again for another adventure with Detective Doodad and the Doodad Gang! Detective Doodad is away on errands. Mindi Lee, the newest member of the team, gets to know Keona and Tony as they tune up the Detective's jetpack. Little do they know they're about to receive a visit from the evil Dr. D. Seaver!

[End music. Keona and Mindi Lee enter. The girls begin working on the jetpack.]

Keona: You've seen the Great Wall of China?

Mindi Lee: Oh, yes. My grandfather took me.

Keona: I'm glad you're part of our team, Mindi Lee. Don't get me wrong—I like being around the boys…

Tony: *[Sarcastically, as he enters from the opposite side]* And we just love being around you too, Keona!

Keona: …but it's nice to have another girl around. Hand me that plug, please?

Mindi Lee: *[Hands Keona a part]* Here you go.

Keona: There're so many adjustments on this jetpack. I'm not sure if I can remember them all.

Mindi Lee: Don't worry, Keona. I've been watching very carefully, and you've done everything exactly the way the Detective showed you.

Keona: Looks like we need a new air filter. *[Keona and Mindi Lee start to exit.]* Tony, we're going to get a filter for the jetpack. We'll be right back. Don't forget what Detective Doodad said: "Don't open the door to strangers for any reason!" Got it?

[Keona and Mindi Lee exit.]

Tony: Yeah, I got it. *[Pause. The doorbell rings. Tony goes to the back edge of the stage.]* Who is it?

Dr. D. Seaver: *[Offstage]* My name is Dr. D. Seaver. I'm an old friend of Detective Doodad's. May I come in?

Tony: I'm not supposed to open the door for strangers.

Dr. D. Seaver: *[Offstage]* Dear boy, I'm not a stranger. I'm one of Detective Doodad's oldest friends. Please—it'll only take a moment.

Tony: Can I take a message?

Dr. D. Seaver: No, but you can take this package I brought for the Detective.

Tony: *[To himself]* Hmmm…what do I do? I know Detective Doodad said not to open the door for anyone I don't know, but this guy is never going to leave. Besides, he said he was a friend of Detective Doodad.

Dr. D. Seaver: *[Impatiently]* Well, kid? What are you waiting for? This package is getting heavy!

Tony: *[Still to himself]* I know! I'll open the door just for a second and grab the package. Nobody even has to know!

[Tony goes to open the door. Dr. D. Seaver enters, carrying box.]

Tony: You can leave the package right there.

Dr. D. Seaver: *[Sets package down]* Thank you, dear boy. I was hoping to see my old friend.

Tony: Sorry, you just missed him.

Dr. D. Seaver: Who said anything about missing him? *[Pats the package]* I'm sure he'll get the point! *[Snickers in a sinister way]*

Tony: OK. See you later, Dr. D. Seaver.

Dr. D. Seaver: Maybe…or maybe not! Ha ha! *[Exits]*

[Keona and Mindi Lee enter.]

Keona: Tony, who was that at the door?

Mindi Lee: And where did this package come from?

Tony: A delivery guy, that's all.

Keona: Tony, Detective Doodad told us not to open the door for anybody.

Tony: It was nothing, OK? He set it down and left.

Mindi Lee: You should never accept anything from strangers. Besides, this package looks suspicious.

Keona: I think we should go to the lab and call the Detective.

Tony: But it's not that big a deal.

[Keona and Mindi Lee exit with Tony. Detective Doodad enters.]

Detective Doodad: Hey, I'm back everyone! *[Spots the package]* What's this? A package. It's such a beautiful day outside; I think I'll open it on the patio! *[Exits with the package]*

[Keona and Mindi Lee enter.]

Mindi Lee: The Detective hasn't answered his phone. He must have his hands full.

Keona: Hey! Where's the package?

Detective Doodad: *[Enters]* Hello, girls. Have you seen my scissors?

[A large explosion rocks the stage. Detective Doodad and the girls are shaken. Tony enters, appearing disheveled.]

Keona: Tony, are you OK?

Tony: I'm fine, but the patio's going to need an extreme makeover. What happened?

Detective Doodad: Wait a minute! That package—where did it come from?

Mindi Lee: Tony accepted it from a deliveryman.

Tony: Not exactly. He said he was an old friend of yours, Dr. D. Seaver.

Detective Doodad: *[Looking surprised]* Dr. D. Seaver? Impossible! Whoever it was, Tony, I'm disappointed that you didn't follow my directions while I was away. You knew I told you not to open the door for anyone.

Tony: I didn't know he was a maniac!

Detective Doodad: Well, of course you didn't. That's why you need to trust me and always follow my instructions.

Tony: I'm sorry for putting everyone in danger, Detective Doodad.

Detective Doodad: I know, Tony, and I forgive you. Let's just thank the Lord that His protection kept us from any harm.

Keona: Yeah!

Detective Doodad: C'mon, everyone, we've got to call the police…

[All exit. Begin music.]

Announcer: *[Offstage]* Well, kids, as you can see, by disobeying Detective Doodad, Tony put everyone in danger. When we decide to do something wrong when we know what's right, it's very dangerous. Will the Doodad Gang learn a lesson from this scary mistake? Stay tuned to their continuing adventures to find out!

[Fade music.]

LESSON 5

Detective Doodad and the Mysterious Message

Genesis 17:1-10, 15-22   Abraham and Sarah Have a Child

Focus: Real faith is putting what we know into action. When we act on what God says, we not only do great things for God, but we also foil our enemy's plans to defeat us.

Characters:

Detective Doodad: a brilliant yet eccentric detective who somehow always has the right answer.
Henry: a younger boy who looks tough, but is gentle. Give him a computer, and he'll find your answer in no time.
Keona: a sensible and intelligent girl who likes to work things out.
Dr. D. Seaver: Detective Doodad's childhood friend and present-day archenemy, a master of disguise.

Props: Magnifying glass, yearbook and CD jewel case with disc.

The Setup: Detective Doodad's library.

[Begin music.]

Announcer: *[Offstage]* Welcome, boys and girls, to the continuing adventures of Detective Doodad and the Doodad Gang! In our last episode, after narrowly avoiding a pyrotechnic package from the evil Dr. D. Seaver, the Doodad Gang began searching for clues to help them foil their enemy's plans. Today we find Henry and the Detective in the library, doing research.

[Fade music. Detective Doodad and Henry enter.]

Henry: *[Reading]* Wow! Detective Doodad, did you know there's a guy in India with a mustache 10 feet long?

Detective Doodad: That's amazing, Henry, but remember: We're here to find out all we can about Dr. D. Seaver, not world records for facial hair.

Henry: Oh, yeah. *[Picks up yearbook]* Hey, isn't this your old yearbook from school?

Detective Doodad: Goodness gracious, it is! I haven't seen that in years. Go, go, Doodad Magnifying Glass! *[He opens the book.]* Aha! I think I've found who we're looking for.

Henry: Douglas Seaver? Is he related to Dr. D. Seaver?

Detective Doodad: If my hunch is correct, he is Dr. D. Seaver. But something awful must have happened to cause him to choose a life of crime.

Henry: Maybe we should send his picture to the rest of the team, Detective, so they'll know what he looks like.

Detective Doodad: Good thinking, Henry, but it won't be that easy. Even in school, he was a master of disguise. He could make himself appear to be almost anyone!

[Keona *enters, carrying a jewel case in one hand.*]

Keona: Detective Doodad! Henry!

Detective Doodad: What do you have there, Keona?

Keona: It's another delivery from Dr. D. Seaver!

Henry: Be careful, Keona. It might be booby-trapped.

Keona: Don't worry, Henry. It's safe. Mindi Lee and I ran it through the scanners before we even touched it.

Detective Doodad: [*Looking at the disc*] It appears to be a holographic videodisc. Put it in the 3-D video player, Keona. I think we're about to get a good look at the evil Dr. D. Seaver.

[Keona *puts the disc down and touches some imaginary controls.* Dr. D. Seaver *enters. A special lighting effect, such as flashlights waving across him or a blue spotlight would help create the holographic effect.*]

Henry: Look out, Detective! It's him. Let's get out of here!

Detective Doodad: Hold on, Henry. It's just a holographic image. Well, well, so it is my old buddy, Douglas Seaver.

Dr. D. Seaver: That's Dr. D. Seaver to you! Long time, no see, Detective. So sorry I "missed" you the other day. But don't worry; I'll make up for it.

Henry: You leave Detective Doodad alone! He's going to catch you anyway!

Dr. D. Seaver: Oh, how touching. Your little pets are so amusing, Doodad. But I'm afraid their faith in you is misplaced. You're good at pulling can openers out of your hat, but it'll take more than that to catch me!

Detective Doodad: Spare me the insults, "Doctor." What do you want?

Dr. D. Seaver: To let you know you should give up now, Detective. You're already beaten; you just don't know it yet. I know everything about your precious Doodad Gang, and there's no way you can stop me.

Keona: Detective Doodad will find a way. You wait and see, Dr. D. Seaver.

Dr. D. Seaver: Oh dear, sweet, little girl; shouldn't you be playing on a swing set somewhere? I'm afraid you're terribly mistaken. The only thing I'll be seeing is my triumph over all of you. I'm warning you, Doodad: Stay out my way—or else! [*Dr. D. Seaver exits quickly.*]

Henry: Oh, no. This is hopeless, Detective! How are we ever going to beat Dr. D. Seaver?

Detective Doodad: Come on, gang! We've got work to do! Dr. D. Seaver doesn't know everything; he's just trying to scare us. If he can make us afraid, he knows we won't stay on the case. God wants us to trust in Him and give it all we've got!

Keona: I'm not going to be afraid of him,

because I don't have to be. I know we'll find a way.

Henry: Me, too! I'm ready for action to defeat this dismal deceiver. What do we need to do, Detective?

Detective Doodad: That's the spirit! First, we need to get this disc back to the lab so we can start analyzing it. Watch out, Dr. D. Seaver! The Doodad Gang is on your trail!

[Everyone exits. Begin music.]

Announcer: *[Offstage]* Wow! It sounds like the Gang is on the right track toward defeating Dr. D. Seaver! They're trusting Detective Doodad and following his orders. When we put our faith in God, we too can foil our enemy's plans. Stay tuned for the continuing adventures of Detective Doodad and the Doodad Gang to see if they can stop the evil Dr. D. Seaver!

[Fade music.]

LESSON 6

Climb Every Mountain

Genesis 22:1–19   Abraham and Isaac at the Altar of Sacrifice

Focus: When the going gets tough in life, how do we react? What's our attitude when challenges come our way? The only real choice is to do the right thing and obey God.

Characters:
  Rusty: a "gung-ho," outdoorsy type, confident and upbeat.
  Wembley: a bit of a whiner. He's not comfortable being outdoors.

Props: Backpacks and walking sticks (optional).

The Setup: Hiking trail in the mountains.

[Begin music.]

Announcer: Ahhh! How I love the great outdoors! Take in that fresh mountain air! Oh—hi kids. Glad you could join me! Do you like to hike? I sure do! Hmm. Looks like Rusty and Wembley are on a hike too, and they're headed this way!

[Fade music. Rusty *and* Wembley *enter.]*

Rusty: Ah, what a beautiful day in the mountains. Look at those snow-covered peaks across the valley—incredible! Feel the wind as it whips through your hair—exhilarating! Smell those wildflowers in bloom—intoxicating!

Wembley: *[Staggering onto the stage]* Collapse in agony as your lungs scream for more air—excruciating! *[Coughs and collapses onto the stage]*

Rusty: Ha ha! What a kidder you are, Wembley. This hiking trip is fun, isn't it?

Wembley: *[Still panting]* Seemed like a good idea at the time, Rusty. But then again, I was sitting in my comfy chair, next to my warm, soft bed, drinking my Big Slurp and eating a hot dog in my jammies. *[Dreamily]* It seems like it was only yesterday!

Rusty: That's because it was yesterday.

Wembley: All I want to know is, are we there yet?

Rusty: Almost, Wembley! It's only five more miles to Eagle Ridge. Then the real fun starts.

Wembley: *[Weakly]* Oh, joy!

Rusty: The rocky climb up Dead Man's Point, the jagged cliffs of Desperation Break, and then finally—

Wembley: *[Interrupts]* —we go home and

watch the game on the big screen?

Rusty: No! Then we begin our assault on the north face of Mount Endeavor!

Wembley: Rusty, I don't think it's such a good idea to go assaulting a mountain. It's a lot bigger than we are.

Rusty: I'm sure it'll throw everything it can at us. Rain, sleet, wind, snow…

Wembley: Are we on vacation, or trying to deliver the mail?

Rusty: The point is, Wembley, no matter what challenges we face, we're going to face them head on.

Wembley: I've had enough challenges for one trip, thank you. That rock under my sleeping bag last night, for instance. Not to mention my sunburn.

Rusty: I tried to tell you that bottle was cooking oil, not sunscreen.

Wembley: How could I tell the difference? The rainstorm washed the labels off everything in my backpack. Now I don't know what's for dinner. We could be having anything from pot roast to pineapples.

Rusty: You have to be prepared for everything up here, Wembley.

Wembley: Well, I wasn't prepared for the mosquitoes. They're gigantic! I tied my tent to the ground so they wouldn't fly off with it.

Rusty: It does take a special kind of person to survive in the wilderness!

Wembley: Rusty, you really do love all this outdoor stuff. Let me ask you something: How can you be so upbeat and cheerful in the face of everything we've gone through to get here?

Rusty: Because I know the right thing to do in any situation we might face. Through careful study, training and a lot of practice, I know what works and what doesn't.

Wembley: You mean there are right ways and wrong ways to climb a mountain?

Rusty: Absolutely! There are hundreds of ways to get into trouble out here. You have to keep making the right choices if you want to succeed. Anyone who doesn't learn to obey the rules of climbing will find himself in trouble real quick. You know that storm last night?

Wembley: Yeah, it came out of nowhere.

Rusty: What would have happened if we'd been on the mountain when that storm hit?

Wembley: We'd be toast!

Rusty: Exactly, Wembley. You don't climb a mountain in the middle of a storm.

Wembley: Not if you want to live!

Rusty: You have to get out of the storm and find shelter. That's why the rules are there in the first place. They're for our safety and protection, not to keep us from having fun.

It's a lot like obeying God. God is our shelter in times of trouble. It's only by obeying His Word and relying on His power that we can weather storms of life.

Wembley: Any other choice will leave you "all wet."

Rusty: Absolutely! Hey, let's get a move on. We're burning daylight.

Wembley: Uh, Rusty, I can think of a better reason to get moving.

Rusty: And what reason would that be?

Wembley: That grizzly bear over there, with the hungry look in his eye.

Rusty: Good enough for me. Let's get out of here!

[Both exit.]

Wembley: *[Offstage]* Rusty, I wonder why the bear came over to the mountain?

Rusty: *[Offstage]* To see what he could see, I guess...

[Begin music.]

Announcer: *[Offstage]* Hey, kids! Hiking seems like hard work, doesn't it? Good thing Rusty knew what to do in those tough situations. There are many tough situations that we face, and they don't have to be while hiking! We need to remember that we will get through those hard times if we obey God, no matter what!

[Fade music.]

LESSON 8

The Doodad Gang and the Case of the Perilous Park Patron

Genesis 37   *The Story of Joseph*

Focus: When trouble comes, our first response is often fear or despair. But God uses hardship to help us become the people He wants us to be. Adversity is an opportunity to grow.

Characters:

Detective Doodad: a brilliant yet eccentric detective who somehow always has the right answer.

Tony: a natural leader who tends to jump in with both feet.

Mindi Lee: the new girl in town. She's seemingly shy, but not afraid to fight for what's right.

Dr. D. Seaver: Detective Doodad's childhood friend and present-day archenemy, a master of disguise.

Props: Shawl. (Dr. D. Seaver could "appear" as an elderly woman puppet or have the shawl around him.)

The Setup: City Park.

[Begin music.]

Announcer: *[Offstage]* Detective Doodad and the Doodad Gang continue their adventure to find out what the evil Dr. D. Seaver is up to! Tony, Mindi Lee and the Detective are hot on his trail. While they follow him to City Park, the cunning criminal has eluded them by blending in with the crowd. Let's join our heroes as they search for Dr. D. Seaver…

[Fade music. Tony, Mindi Lee and Detective Doodad enter.]

Tony: Dr. D. Seaver was right in front of us, Detective Doodad. Now he's gone!

Mindi Lee: It's like he disappeared. But we know that's not possible.

Detective Doodad: That's right, Mindi Lee. Dr. D. Seaver has obviously used one of his disguises to throw us off track.

Mindi Lee: That means he's still here in City Park.

Detective Doodad: Exactly. We're going to have to split up and search the park. I want you two to stick together.

Tony: But Detective, we're never going to find him.

Detective Doodad: Don't give up, Tony. I know this is difficult, but remember: God uses hard times to help us grow, so don't lose heart. And be careful—Dr. D. Seaver is a master of disguise. You might talk to him without even knowing it! *[Exits]*

Tony: This is like looking for a needle in a haystack.

Mindi Lee: People really look for needles in haystacks? Why don't they just go buy a new needle?

17

Tony: It's an expression, Mindi Lee. It means doing something the hard way.

Mindi Lee: My father says that sometimes the hard way is the only way.

Tony: I guess. Let's search the other side of the park, OK?

Mindi Lee: OK! I'm sure there are more haystacks over there.

[Tony and Mindi Lee exit. They re-enter on the other side of the stage.]

Tony: How are we going to find Dr. D. Seaver when we don't know what he looks like? This is so hard!

Mindi Lee: Don't give up, Tony. Remember what Detective Doodad said? "God uses the hard times to help us grow."

Tony: I guess I can practice my interviewing skills.

Mindi Lee: Tony, that's it! We don't know what Dr. D. Seaver looks like, but we do know what he's like. If we talk to people, and he's in disguise…

Tony: Maybe he'll reveal himself!

[Tony and Mindi Lee exit. Searching music plays. They re-enter.]

Tony: We're getting nowhere.

Mindi Lee: No one said this was going to be easy, Tony. We've talked to at least 43 people who aren't evil geniuses.

[Dr. D. Seaver, disguised as an elderly woman, enters.]

Tony: The only person left is that old lady. Here goes nothing. *[Crosses to woman]* Excuse me, ma'am. Could we talk to you?

Dr. D. Seaver: *[Covered with shawl, and with a disguised voice]* Certainly, I love talking to young people. Why do you look so tired?

Tony: We've been chasing a suspect. I think we should give up and head home.

Dr. D. Seaver: I think you should give up, too. There's no reason for you to be running around on some hopeless chase.

Mindi Lee: I don't mean any disrespect, ma'am, but it's not hopeless. Detective Doodad asked us to help.

Dr. D. Seaver: Detective Doodad? Isn't he that bumbling investigator who tells his little helpers what to do?

Mindi Lee: He doesn't just tell us what to do. The Detective helps us. He knows that God will help us in the hard times, too.

Dr. D. Seaver: I'm afraid the Detective has been lying to you, dear. He knows that God won't help you, especially in the hard times. The Detective only says these things to get you to do his dirty work.

Tony: *[Thinking]* He has been working us pretty hard.

Mindi Lee: *[Talks into wrist]* Detective! It's

Mindi Lee. Please come! We need your help!

Dr. D. Seaver: That's right, precious boy. The defective Detective is using you!

Mindi Lee: Don't listen to her, Tony. It's really Dr. D. Seaver!

Tony: She's right! I recognize your voice.

Dr. D. Seaver: *[Ducks down below stage and pops back up as* Dr. D. Seaver.*]* Then you should also recognize when you've been beaten! You found me, but you'll never catch me! But don't cry…I'll be back! *[Laughs and exits]*

Detective Doodad: *[Enters]* Tony! Mindi Lee! You found him! You didn't give up, no matter how hard it got. I'm proud of both of you. Now let's go catch Dr. D. Seaver before he can spread any more lies.

[Detective Doodad, Tony *and* Mindi Lee *exit. Begin music.]*

Announcer: *[Offstage]* Wow! Kids, can you believe they found Dr. D. Seaver? Even though it was hard to track him down, they were able to because they didn't give up. God encourages us to be like the Doodad Gang and not give up during hard times. These hard times give us the opportunity to grow! Stay tuned for the continuing adventures of Detective Doodad and the Doodad Gang to find out if they can catch Dr. D. Seaver!

[Fade music.]

LESSON 9

The Doodad Gang Spreads the News

Exodus 3:1-22

The Call of Moses

Focus: It's up to us to share the good news we've received. All Christians can share their stories about coming to know God, as well as the truth they've learned from getting to know Him.

Characters:

Detective Doodad: a brilliant yet eccentric detective who somehow always has the right answer.
Henry: a younger boy who looks tough, but is gentle. Give him a computer, and he'll find your answer in no time.
Keona: a sensible and intelligent girl who likes to work things out.
Dr. D. Seaver: Detective Doodad's childhood friend and present-day archenemy, a master of disguise.

Props: Baseball cap (Dr. D. Seaver's disguise) and small flashlight (strapped to Doodad's hand as the Doodad Deceiver Revealer).

The Setup: The neighborhood.

[Begin music.]

Announcer: *[Offstage]* It's time again for the continuing adventures of Detective Doodad and the Doodad Gang! The Detective has invented an amazing device to expose Dr. D. Seaver's disguises. While making the finishing touches, the Doodad Gang has spread across the city to tell everyone the good news.

[Fade music. Henry enters.]

Detective Doodad: *[Offstage]* Remember, I need each of you to tell as many people as you can about my latest invention, the Doodad Deceiver Revealer. This device can see through Dr. D. Seaver's disguises.

Henry: *[Speaking into wrist]* But Detective Doodad, what if people don't believe me?

Detective Doodad: *[Offstage]* Don't worry about that, Henry. Your job is to share the good news. Detective Doodad, over and out!

Henry: *[To himself]* Oh, brother. Detective Doodad wants me to tell people about his discovery. I get nervous when I have to talk to people. What will I say? How will I know what to do?

Keona: *[Enters]* Hi, Henry!

Henry: Hi, Keona. *[Looking down]*

Keona: Why do you look so sad? We have great news to share!

Henry: I know; It's just...I don't think I'm the right person for this job.

Keona: Why do you say that?

Henry: I'm not as good a leader as Tony is. People listen to him. And I don't know as much as you and Mindi Lee.

Keona: Yes you do! You've seen Dr. D. Seaver. You know how important it is for us to stop his lies.

Henry: Yes, but why do I have to go?

Keona: Because people need to hear what you have to say, Henry.

Henry: Maybe I should wait until I am older.

Keona: Henry, there's no time to waste. The longer you wait, the more people will fall under Dr. D. Seaver's lies. You don't have to put on a show. Just share what you know is true.

Henry: *[Thinking]* Tell them what I know to be true!

Keona: Be confident, Henry. You're a messenger of the truth. *[Exits]*

Henry: I am a messenger of the truth! Yeah!

[Dr. D. Seaver, disguised as a boy in a baseball cap, enters.]

Henry: Hi, I'm Henry. What's your name?

Dr. D. Seaver: *[With a thinly disguised voice]* You can call me Doug.

Henry: I've got some really good news, Doug. Have you heard?

Dr. D. Seaver: Heard what?

Henry: About Dr. D. Seaver.

Dr. D. Seaver: I heard he's not such a bad guy, once you get to know him.

Henry: Well, I've seen him, and believe me, he is a bad guy. Anyway, Detective Doodad has found a way to reveal Dr. D. Seaver!

Dr. D. Seaver: No kidding! That's interesting news...how do you know about it?

Henry: I'm a messenger of the truth!

Dr. D. Seaver: No, you're not. You're not a messenger; you're just a goof!

Henry: *[Indignant]* But I am a messenger of the truth.

Dr. D. Seaver: *[Mocking]* You're not a messenger; you're just a goof! You're not a messenger; you're just a goof! Ha, ha, ha!

Henry: You can make fun of me, but that doesn't change the truth. And speaking of what's true, you sound familiar... *[Speaks into wrist]* Detective Doodad! It's Henry. Trace my signal and come quick!

Dr. D. Seaver: The Doodad Gang thinks you're a goof, too.

Henry: No, they don't. They're my friends.

Dr. D. Seaver: They told me they think you're the goofiest person in the whole world.

Henry: That's not true, and I know it!

Dr. D. Seaver: Oh, really? How can you be so sure?

Henry: Because I know the truth. Isn't that right, Detective Doodad?

Detective Doodad: *[Enters]* That's right, Henry.

Dr. D. Seaver: Doodad? What's he doing here?

Henry: He's here to shine the light of truth on you, Dr. D. Seaver.

Dr. D. Seaver: But…but…I'm just a little boy!

Detective Doodad: We'll soon find out! Go, go, Doodad Deceiver Revealer!

Dr. D. Seaver: No, not my disguise!

[Flashlight shines on the boy, who falls out of sight.]

Dr. D. Seaver: *[Re-enters as his true self.]* So, I see you have a new toy!

Detective Doodad: And I see you're still up to your old tricks.

Dr. D. Seaver: It almost worked…except for that meddler, Henry. I'll get you for this! *[Exits quickly]*

Henry: Thanks, Detective. You got here just in time.

Detective Doodad: No, thank you, Henry. You stood up to Dr. D. Seaver. You even saw through his lies. Even though you're young, you can still be a powerful messenger for the truth.

Henry: I'm going to tell everyone!

[Detective Doodad and Henry exit. Begin music.]

Announcer: *[Offstage]* Way to go, Henry! Even though he's young, Henry was able to foil Dr. D. Seaver's plans and share the truth. Will Henry help the Doodad Gang put an end to Dr. D. Seaver's evil ways? Stay tuned to the continuing adventures of Detective Doodad and the Doodad Gang to find out!

[Fade music.]

LESSON 10

Special Delivery

Exodus 12:1–13   The Story of Passover

Focus: God protects His people. When the death angel passed over the homes of Egypt, God protected the Israelites from harm. Just as good packaging protects valuable contents, Jesus protects us from sin and death.

Characters:
  Rachel: Tommy's twin sister. She is thoughtful and well-spoken.
  Tommy: Rachel's twin brother, who loves to joke around.

Props: Small piece of black posterboard (pinned to Rachel's hand as the Palm Pad), beat-up cardboard box, wrapping paper, bubble wrap and Styrofoam packing peanuts.

The Setup: The living room.

[Begin music.]

Announcer: *[Offstage]* Welcome, kids! It's time for a birthday…well, actually, two birthdays! Our story today is about the twins, Rachel and Tommy, who will learn something new from a box—that's right, I said a box! See if you can tell what it is!

[Fade music. Tommy enters.]

Tommy: This is going to be the best birthday ever! I'm going to have my friends over; I'm going to get a bunch of really cool presents, and then I'm going to play with them until my fingers fall off!

Rachel: *[Enters]* Excuse me, dear brother, but aren't you forgetting something?

Tommy: *[Thinking]* Oh yeah, I'm going to eat cake until my tongue turns yellow!

Rachel: No, that's not what I was talking about.

Tommy: You're going to sing "Happy Birthday" to me and move to Siberia?

Rachel: Very funny. I was talking about the fact that it's my birthday, too!

Tommy: *[Amazed]* What? Your birthday's the same day as my birthday? Oh no, Rachel! How in the world did that happen?

Rachel: *[Frustrated]* Tommy! For being a twin brother, you're really weird.

Tommy: I'm weird enough to be a regular brother! It's just that I'm excited about the party tomorrow. Have we gotten Grandma and Grandpa's package yet? They always send our presents together.

Rachel: Let me check my Palm Pad for gifts. *[She looks at the object pinned to her hand.]* G… G… where is it? Groceries, greeting cards…

Tommy: Oh, brother! I'll check the front

porch. *[Tommy goes out; we hear a door open and close, and then he returns with a damaged box.]* Hey Rachel, look what I found!

Rachel: *[Notices damaged box]* A crushed box?

Tommy: It's Grandma and Grandpa's package!

Rachel: Hooray! Our presents are here! But what happened to the box?

Tommy: It looks like an elephant sat on it! *[Sets the box behind stage]*

Rachel: And then used it for a toothbrush.

Tommy: We better open it to make sure nothing's broken.

Rachel: Well, Mom did say it was OK to open any packages from family. Still, maybe we should wait…

Tommy: Do you really want to wait until tomorrow to find out if your present is in one piece?

Rachel: Good point. We better open it. *[Kids lean over as if opening the box.]*

[Sound of a box being opened. Wrapping paper, Styrofoam peanuts and bubble wrap fly up from below.]

Tommy: Bubble wrap! I love bubble wrap! *[Sound of bubble wrap popping]* Ooooh, popcorn! *[Peanuts fly up.]*

Rachel: Looks like Grandma wrapped these presents really well.

Tommy: Grandma sure does like tape! *[More wrapping flies up.]*

Rachel: Cool, Tommy! Nothin's broken! Look what we got!

Tommy: Awesome! I got a Super Soaker Water Blaster!

Rachel: And I got an American Gal doll! Just what I wanted! Grandma, you're terrific!

Tommy: But this box is history.

Rachel: That box really took a beating, but my doll came out without a scratch!

Tommy: Rachel, I have a new respect for the lowly cardboard box. Just think about it: One day you're all nice and sturdy, and then the next day somebody slaps tape on you and throws you in a truck.

Rachel: You bounce across the country, getting dinged up with the other packages. Finally, you arrive at your destination, all bruised and beat-up.

Tommy: After all that hard work, they throw you away and keep the stuff on the inside!

When you think about it, though, that's the whole purpose of being a box: to keep the stuff on the inside safe.

Rachel: Yeah… *[Abruptly]* Tommy, this may sound strange, but this box reminds me of Passover!

Tommy: Pass what over?

Rachel: Remember? In church we learned about the Israelites and how God protected them at Passover.

Tommy: I remember that. The children of Israel put lamb's blood on their houses, and the angel of death passed right over them.

Rachel: God protected His children by the blood of the lamb, like this box protected our presents.

Tommy: I think this week our teacher said we'd learn about how Jesus is the Passover Lamb.

Rachel: Right! He's our protection from sin and death!

Tommy: God protects people really well. He doesn't even need tape!

Rachel: I bet the Israelites were really happy about their "special delivery."

Tommy: Just like I'm happy about ours. This is going to be the best birthday ever, Rachel.

Rachel: Yeah! Let's go call Grandma and Grandpa and thank them for the presents!

Tommy: OK, but on one condition.

Rachel: What's that?

Tommy: I get to talk first. That way, you can "wrap it up!"

Rachel: Oh, please! Someone "deliver me!"

[Rachel and Tommy exit. Begin music.]

Announcer: *[Offstage]* Hey, kids! Have you ever gotten a present in the mail that had been banged around like Rachel's and Tommy's? It's amazing how that cardboard box protects what's inside! Just like that cardboard box, God protects us. He surrounds us with His love and keeps us from sin and death.

[Fade music.]

LESSON 12

Detective Doodad vs. the Decepto-Bots

Numbers 13:17—14:6   The Report of the Twelve

Focus: There's an old saying: "I won't believe it until I see it with my own eyes." Many people trust their senses more than they trust God. We need to learn how to look at life the way God looks at it.

Characters:

Dr. D. Seaver: Detective Doodad's childhood friend and present-day archenemy, a master of disguise.
Detective Doodad: a brilliant yet eccentric detective who somehow always has the right answer.
Tony: a natural leader who tends to jump in with both feet.
Keona: a sensible and intelligent girl who likes to work things out.
Henry: a younger boy who looks tough, but is gentle. Give him a computer, and he'll find your answer in no time.
Mindi Lee: the new girl in town. She's seemingly shy, but not afraid to fight for what's right.

Props: Several cardboard rectangles made from shoebox lids, with craft stick "arms" (as the Decepto-Bots), one flashlight per "robot" and sunglasses.

The Setup: City streets at night. Turn off or dim the lights.

[Begin music.]

Announcer: *[Offstage]* It's time once again for the continuing adventures of Detective Doodad and the Doodad Gang! A dark night has fallen upon Techno City. The evil Dr. D. Seaver has unleashed a horde of "Decepto-Bots." Though small, the Decepto-Bots project a powerful hologram that makes them appear gigantic. People flee in terror before them. Fortunately, Detective Doodad has turned his laser pointer into a pair of Z-ray sunglasses that reveal the robots' true size. Unfortunately, there's only one pair! Join us now as we catch up to the Doodad Gang, deep in the heart of the city.

[Fade music. Lights should be dim or out. Dr. D. Seaver enters. A flashlight illuminates his face.]

Dr. D. Seaver: All my plans are falling into place! My army of Decepto-Bots has cleared the streets, paving the way for me to steal and plunder. Ha, ha, ha! The police are helpless; who can stand against the great Dr. D. Seaver? *[Exits]*

[The shadows of two Decepto-Bots cross the back curtain or wall of the stage. Holding the flashlight in front of the robot cutout creates a large shadow. Detective Doodad, Tony, Keona, Henry *and* Mindi Lee *enter. Flashlights and robot shadows help illuminate them.]*

Tony: The robots are everywhere, Detective Doodad!

Keona: They're enormous.

Mindi Lee: At least 15 feet tall, by my calculations.

Henry: How are we going to stop them?

[Several robot shadows appear and pass by.]

Detective Doodad: Cheer up, gang, things aren't as bad as they seem. The Police Commissioner has asked for our help, and that's what we're going to give him.

Tony: But Detective, what can we do against a bunch of giant killer robots?

Detective Doodad: That's just it, Tony. They're not giants at all. The problem is, you can't see what I see.

Keona: What do you mean, Detective?

Detective Doodad: All you can see is their appearance, Keona. But it's a lie. My Doodad Z-ray sunglasses help me see the Decepto-Bots as they really are—tiny and weak. Why, you could break one by simply stepping on it.

Henry: Wait a second. Are you saying we can walk up to one of those monsters and just step on it?

Detective Doodad: That's exactly what I'm saying, Henry.

Mindi Lee: It all makes sense. If the robots are projecting a false image, that might explain why they aren't actually attacking us.

[Robot shadows cross the stage.]

Detective Doodad: Exactly, Mindi Lee. It's an elaborate deception, cooked up by that master of mischief, Dr. D. Seaver. I'm asking you to help me show the people of Techno City that there's nothing to be afraid of. Now, who's with me?

Tony: I am!

Mindi Lee: Me, too!

Henry: Count me in!

Keona: I'll bring dessert! *[They all look at her.]* Hey, I figured we might get hungry.

[The entire gang exits. Robot shadows fill the stage.]

Announcer: *[Enters]* Detective Doodad dispatched the Doodad Gang to every corner of the city. Trusting in their hero and knowing he would never lead them astray, Tony, Keona, Henry and Mindi Lee prepared to battle the Decepto-Bots! *[Exits]*

[Tony and Keona enter. Two shadows dance on the walls.]

Tony: Ready, Keona?

Keona: Ready as I'll ever be, Tony. I'll take the closer one, OK?

Tony: OK. On your mark, get set, go!

Both: Aaaagh! Take that, you robots!

[Tony and Keona jump out and stomp the robots, then exit.]

Announcer: *[Enters]* As Tony and Keona smashed the robots, Mindi Lee and Henry find themselves surrounded. *[Exits]*

[Henry and Mindi Lee enter, with shadows all around.]

Henry: It looks like we're surrounded.

Announcer: *[Offstage]* I just said that.

Henry: Oh, sorry.

Mindi Lee: If what the Detective said is true, it shouldn't make a difference.

Henry: Those robots sure look big, but I'm not going to doubt Detective Doodad now. Let's get them!

Both: Aaaaah! Here we come!

[Henry and Mindi Lee stomp the robots, then exit. Begin music.]

Announcer: *[Offstage]* And so the Doodad Gang stomped and smashed their way across Techno City, until all of the Decepto-Bots were defeated. Detective Doodad earned the gratitude of a thankful city, and the Doodad Gang learned once again the power of living in the light of truth. That's always what happens when we see things as God sees them!

[Fade music.]

LESSON 13

Detective Doodad and the Dangerous Devices Department

Joshua 3:1-17   Joshua Leads Into the Promised Land

Focus: God has given us many blessings, which the enemy will often try to take away. It's our job to stand up and fight for what God has given to us and to defend the truth of His Word. His power will cause us to win in the end!

Characters:

Detective Doodad: a brilliant yet eccentric detective who somehow always has the right answer.
Keona: a sensible and intelligent girl who likes to work things out.
Dr. D. Seaver: Detective Doodad's childhood friend and present-day archenemy, a master of disguise.

Props: Glasses and mustache (disguise for Dr. D. Seaver), and papers.

The Setup: City Hall, then a janitor's closet.

[Begin music.]

Announcer: *[Offstage]* It's time again for the continuing adventures of Detective Doodad and the Doodad Gang! Answering a mysterious summons to the Techno City Dangerous Devices Department, Detective Doodad and Keona head to City Hall…

[Fade music. Detective Doodad and Keona enter.]

Keona: Wow! I never knew City Hall was so big, Detective Doodad.

Detective Doodad: And it seems to be getting bigger all the time, Keona. I've been here hundreds of times, but I've never heard of the Dangerous Devices Department.

Keona: It's not on the map.

Detective Doodad: And there's no phone number.

[Dr. D. Seaver, disguised as "Agent Smith," enters.]

Dr. D. Seaver: Detective Doodad. I'm Smith, agent in charge of the Dangerous Devices Department.

Detective Doodad: Good morning, Agent Smith. This is Keona, one of my assistants.

Dr. D. Seaver: Yes, I see that. Detective Doodad, I believe I asked you to come alone.

Detective Doodad: Yes, you did, but I've found that having a friend to help you is always better than going it alone.

Dr. D. Seaver: *[Annoyed]* Isn't that special?

Keona: We couldn't find your department, Agent Smith.

Dr. D. Seaver: It's a new agency, miss… rather small. But we have some very big plans! I have a few forms you'll need to fill out first, Detective. Please follow me. *[Exits]*

Keona: I don't like the looks of this.

Detective Doodad: Me neither, Keona. Keep your eyes open, OK?

Keona: OK!

[Both exit. Transition music plays. Scene changes to the janitor's closet. Dr. D. Seaver re-enters, holding some papers. Detective Doodad and Keona re-enter next to him.]

Detective Doodad: Nice office, Agent Smith. Was the broom closet already taken?

Keona: This is the broom closet!

Dr. D. Seaver: It's temporary. We're remodeling.

Keona: I sure hope so.

Dr. D. Seaver: Here are 27 more forms you need to fill out.

Keona: Twenty-seven more? But we've been filling out forms for the last three hours!

Detective Doodad: That's right. Even my Doodad Pencil Sharpener is worn out. What's the meaning of all this paperwork, Agent Smith?

Dr. D. Seaver: These are registration forms, Detective, for all those inventions of yours.

Keona: Do you mean the jetpack and the laser pointer and stuff?

Dr. D. Seaver: Precisely.

Keona: Why would Detective Doodad need to register his inventions?

Dr. D. Seaver: Because I've decided that the tools you use are dangerous.

Detective Doodad: Dangerous? They're not dangerous!

Dr. D. Seaver: I'm afraid they are, and in accordance with Section 6, paragraph 6 of the Dangerous Devices Act, all of your instruments will be confiscated.

Keona: Confiscated? You mean you're going to take our tools?

Dr. D. Seaver: Yes.

Keona: But how will the Doodad Gang help people and stop Dr. D. Seaver?

Dr. D. Seaver: That's not my concern, missy. Perhaps you should stop trying to help so many people and mind your own business!

Detective Doodad: This isn't right, Agent Smith. God has given the Doodad Gang the skills and the tools to help others. We're not going to sit here and let you tell us what we can or can't do.

Keona: That's right. We'll fight for what God has given us!

Dr. D. Seaver: God has nothing to do with it, little girl. You'll settle for what I give you, is that clear? If you do as you're told, I might even let you keep your clubhouse!

Keona: Why do we have to settle?

Dr. D. Seaver: Because that's the way things are, and a child like you can't change that.

Keona: But the Detective taught us that with God, all things are possible.

Dr. D. Seaver: That's just a lie they tell boys and girls!

Detective Doodad: The only lie around here is coming from you, Agent Smith. Or should I say, Dr. D. Seaver? *[Detective Doodad pulls off the disguise.]*

Dr. D. Seaver: My disguise! How clever of you, Detective. How did you ever catch on?

Detective Doodad: By keeping my eyes and ears open, and studying the clues: this broom closet, these papers and your phony agency.

Dr. D. Seaver: I almost had your precious inventions, but believe me…I will get them one of these days.

Keona: Our fight isn't with City Hall after all.

Detective Doodad: No, Keona, our fight is with evil and all who serve evil.

Dr. D. Seaver: You may have stopped me this time, Doodad, but my blinding powder will let me escape once again! *[There's a poof sound, and Dr. D. Seaver vanishes.]*

Keona: He's gone!

Detective Doodad: We'll find him. But don't forget what you've seen today. Always stand up to evil, and hold on tight to the things that God has given you!

[Detective Doodad and Keona exit. Begin music.]

Announcer: *[Offstage]* Wow! That Dr. D. Seaver sure is evil, isn't he? Good thing Keona and Detective Doodad remembered to stand up and fight for what God has given them. God's power gave them victory over Dr. D. Seaver! Stay tuned for the continuing adventures of Detective Doodad and the Doodad Gang!

[Fade music.]

LESSON 14

Faith Factor

Judges 6:11–18   The Story of Gideon

Focus: There's only one sure way to overcome the challenges of this world: Jesus Christ. Jesus has won the battle, but it's up to us to live in His victory. If we trust in Him and follow his ways, we can be God's champions.

Characters:
  Alex Winsome: a game-show host.
  Buzzkill Stoneheart: a self-proclaimed spiritual guru.
  Norma Jenkins: a Sunday school teacher.

Props: Small "mountain" (cardboard cutout) and phone receiver on a rod.

The Setup: A game show.

[Begin music.]

Announcer: *[Offstage]* And now it's time for America's spiritual game show, *Faith Factor*, where contestants put their faith to the test to see who will claim the victory. Please welcome your host, Alex Winsome!

[Fade music. Alex enters.]

Alex: Hi everyone, I'm Alex Winsome. Welcome to another round of *Faith Factor*. This is the show where we challenge people's faith head-on to see who really has a grip on the ultimate power in time of need. Let's get started by welcoming our returning champ, Buzzkill Stoneheart!

Buzzkill: *[Enters and struts around]* Hi there, fans! I love ya!

Alex: Welcome back, Buzz.

Buzzkill: Thank you, Alex.

Alex: You've had an exciting ride these last few days. I understand you're writing a book?

Buzzkill: Now that America knows I'm a true spiritual champion, I want to help people through my 89-step program called "Chant Your Way to Victory."

Alex: Yes, that chant came in handy against your opponents. What's your strategy today, Buzz?

Buzzkill: Same as always, Alex. Win at all costs.

Alex: It's a good plan, but today we have a serious competitor. Johnny, tell us a little about her.

Announcer: *[Offstage]* Our next contestant is Norma Jenkins, a Sunday school teacher from Conqueror's Valley. Norma's friends call her a prayer warrior, but she calls herself a born-again follower of Jesus Christ. Please welcome our very first Christian contestant, Norma Jenkins!

[Applause as Norma enters]

Alex: Hi Norma, welcome to our show.

Norma: Hello, Alex.

Alex: So, you're a Christian. What does that mean exactly?

Norma: Well, it means that I've given my heart to Jesus Christ. Because of that, I don't have to worry about facing tough challenges. His power in me is what makes me a champ at this *Faith Factor* stuff! Look out Buzzkill—you're going down for the count!

Audience: Ooh! Ahhh!

Alex: So you're confident your faith in God will overcome today's challenges?

Norma: Absolutely. If God is for me, who can stand against me?

Alex: Powerful words, Buzzkill. What do you have to say to that?

Buzzkill: Enough talk already. Let's rock!

Alex: Johnny, what's the first test?

Announcer: *[Offstage]* To see whose faith is stronger, we're asking our contestants to move this mountain. *[Mountain appears.]*

Alex: Buzz, as our reigning champion, you go first.

Buzzkill: Once again I will summon the awesome power of the cosmic life force deep within me!

Alex: *[To the audience]* I think that means he's going to chant.

Buzzkill: Uh, yes. Oonga Bonga Boygo Boo! Oonga Bonga Boygo Boo! Oonga Boonga Boygo Boo!

Alex: Nothing's happening, champ.

Buzzkill: Hey, this is a lot harder than reading tea leaves. I just need to channel my powers. *[Dances around and groans]* Oonga Boonga Boygo Boo!

[A buzzer sounds.]

Alex: I'm sorry, Buzz, but time's up. Norma, it's your turn. Do you think you can do it?

Norma: I'm sure I can't by myself, Alex. But like I said, Jesus' power will help me do the impossible. *[Praying]* Lord Jesus, I praise You for working in me today. You said that if I have even just a little bitty, teeny tiny, eensy weensy kind of faith—faith as tiny as a mustard seed [see Matthew 17:20], I can tell this mountain to move from here to there, and it will. So I'm counting on You now, Jesus. And by the way, whatever happens, You get all the credit! Amen.

[The mountain rumbles and moves. A bell sounds, and the audience applauds.]

Alex: That was amazing!

Norma: It's not my power, Alex, but the power of Jesus in me…just because I trust Him.

Announcer: *[Offstage]* Our final test today, Alex, is the salvation challenge. Can the faith of our contestants help save a soul from darkness?

Buzzkill: Uh, Alex, I don't understand. Save a soul from what?

Alex: From the darkness of sin, Buzz.

Buzzkill: There's no such thing as sin. However, my chant will save you from bad vibes and parking tickets! Oonga Boonga Boygo Boo!

Alex: *[Sarcastically]* Right! How about you, Norma?

Norma: Well, Alex, salvation only comes from God. But we can pray for others. I've been praying for many people to ask Jesus into their lives, especially my grandson. In fact, I just used my "phone a saint" lifeline to call the prayer chain at church. I can't wait for you to hear what they told me.

[A phone appears.]

Alex: *[Ear to the phone]* Yes? He did? Outstanding! Thank you for the news. Ladies and gentlemen, Norma's grandson has just accepted the Lord. I think we have a new champion!

Audience: *[Applauds]* How'd you do it, Norma?

Norma: I just do what God says to do: trust in Him with all my heart. Jesus is my champion, and He makes me one, too!

[All three exit as audience applauds. Begin music.]

Announcer: That says it all, kids! Jesus is your champion, and He'll make you one, too!

[Fade music.]

LESSON 17

The Doodad Gang and the Capture of the Conniving Doctor

1 Samuel 17:32–50   David and Goliath

Focus: There are times in life when we're afraid, especially when we face problems that seem too big for us. God's Word tells us not to fear. It's our job to stand strong in the faith and be brave for God.

Characters:

Tony: a natural leader who tends to jump in with both feet.
Mindi Lee: the new girl in town. She's seemingly shy, but not afraid to fight for what's right.
Henry: a younger boy who looks tough, but is gentle. Give him a computer, and he'll find your answer in no time.
Dr. D. Seaver: Detective Doodad's childhood friend and present-day archenemy, a master of disguise.

Props: Flashlight (as the Deceiver Revealer) and trap (either a net or a wide ribbon of fabric on two rods).

The Setup: Doodad Gang clubhouse. Dr. D. Seaver appears in this skit disguised as Detective Doodad. Use the Detective Doodad puppet with Dr. D. Seaver's voice for these parts.

[Begin music.]

Announcer: *[Offstage]* It's time again for the continuing adventures of Detective Doodad and the Doodad Gang! Today we find Tony, Henry, and Mindi Lee in the clubhouse. Detective Doodad is away at a crime-fighting conference, but he's called in to leave instructions for the Gang. Little do they know how much they'll need them.

[Fade music. Tony, Mindi Lee and Henry enter.]

Detective Doodad: *[Voice only]* Now, repeat after me: Don't open the door to strangers.

Tony, Mindi Lee, Henry: *[Together]* Don't open the door to strangers!

Detective Doodad: Very good. And remember to be brave for God. Don't worry about the plans of that evil Dr. D. Seaver. Be strong, and don't lose hope. Detective Doodad out!

Tony: Be brave for God. No problem!

Henry: What's the bravest thing you've ever done, Tony?

Tony: Jumping my bike over Rock Creek. I was the only kid in the neighborhood who had the guts to try. How about you, Henry?

Henry: Once I had to guard Billy Thompson in a basketball game. He was big and scary, but I didn't back down.

Tony: What about you, Mindi Lee?

Mindi Lee: *[Thinking]* The bravest thing I've ever done? Asking Jesus into my heart and becoming a Christian.

Henry: Really?

Mindi Lee: Yes. It's not always easy to follow

Jesus. Would you be a Christian if it meant your family didn't like you anymore?

Tony: What do you mean?

Mindi Lee: Where I come from, people pray to their ancestors, not to God. Becoming a Christian in my country is seen as disrespectful to your family. My grandparents were very upset when Mom and Dad became Christians. They said, "Who will pray for us after we die?"

Henry: Wow, I've never heard that before.

Mindi Lee: Some of my relatives still won't talk to us.

Tony: How do you deal with it?

Mindi Lee: We pray for them. Sometimes it hurts to think about it, but I wouldn't trade Jesus for anything.

[The doorbell rings.]

Henry: Who's that?

Tony: Let's find out!

[Tony runs out to get the door.]

Mindi Lee: Remember: Don't open the door to strangers!

[Tony re-enters with Dr. D. Seaver disguised as Detective Doodad.]

Tony: It's not a stranger, it's...

Mindi Lee and Henry: Detective Doodad!

Henry: But I thought you went to a meeting.

Dr. D. Seaver: *[Disguised voice]* I did, Henry, but I came back. There was something important I had to tell you.

Mindi Lee: What is it?

Dr. D. Seaver: I left you the wrong message. I meant to tell you, "Don't be brave for God."

Tony: Don't be brave for God?

Dr. D. Seaver: Yes, Tony. You see, God is all-powerful, so He really doesn't need our help.

Henry: What are we supposed to do, then?

Dr. D. Seaver: Not a thing, Henry. Just sit back and let God do it all by Himself.

Mindi Lee: That doesn't sound like something Detective Doodad would say. He always says that God has something for all of us to do.

Dr. D. Seaver: Now Mindi, who's the Detective here? Trust me—I know what's best.

Mindi Lee: *[Whispers]* Tony! Something's not right.

Tony: Yeah, this smells fishy. I've got the tool kit right here.

Mindi Lee: Detective, I was wondering: Why did you ring the doorbell? Why didn't you just use your key?

Dr. D. Seaver: I, uh, left my keys at the meeting.

Henry: You never forget your keys. Detective.

Mindi Lee: That's right, Henry! Tony—Go, go, Doodad Deceiver Revealer!

Dr. D. Seaver: No!

[Tony shines the flashlight. Dr. D. Seaver sinks below the stage, then reappears as himself.]

Henry: It's Dr. D. Seaver!

Dr. D. Seaver: Yes, and I'm going to get you!

Tony: You don't scare us, Dr. D. Seaver.

Mindi Lee: Yeah, we know something you don't: how to be brave for God. Throw the switch, Tony!

[Tony mimes hitting a switch, and a trap captures Dr. D. Seaver.]

Dr. D. Seaver: A trap? I've been captured by children!

Henry: We got him! We got Dr. D. Seaver!

[The kids exit, leading Dr. D. Seaver. Begin music.]

Announcer: *[Offstage]* And so the Doodad Gang succeeded in capturing Dr. D. Seaver. By standing brave in the face of evil, Tony, Henry and Mindi Lee learned a valuable lesson. Be brave for God, and He'll be there for you!

[Fade music.]

LESSON 18

Wise or Not So Wise

1 Kings 3:5-15   Solomon Asks for Wisdom

Focus: There's a difference between knowledge and wisdom. Knowing the right answers can only take you so far; knowing the wisdom that comes from God is the smart choice.

Characters:

Quinn Allen: a game-show host.
Professor Rudolph Primp: a snooty, know-it-all type.
Wally: a tough construction worker.

Props: Wallet and signs to cue the audience to shout "Wise!" or "Not so Wise!"

The Setup: Game show. Have a helper hold up the appropriate sign to cue the audience during the skit.

[Begin music.]

Announcer: *[Offstage]* Welcome, one and all, to the quiz show that tests your wits, Wise or Not So Wise. This is the show where you decide if the contestant is wise or not so wise! Right now, please welcome your host, Quinn Allen!

[Fade music. Quinn enters.]

Quinn: Hi, everybody. I'm Quinn Allen, and I'm your host for this challenge of choices we like to call *Wise or Not So Wise*. On our program, you get to decide if our players make the wise choice. Let's meet our first contestant right now.

Announcer: *[Offstage]* Quinn, our first contestant today is Professor Rudolph Primp, from Varsityville. He's an associate professor of human studies. Let's see if the Professor is… *[Dramatic voice]* wise or not so wise!

[Audience applauds as Rudolph enters.]

Quinn: Good afternoon, Professor, and welcome to the program.

Rudolph: Thank you, Quinn.

Quinn: As you know, you get rewarded not only for coming up with the right answers to our questions, but also for making the wise choice, as decided by the audience.

Rudolph: *[Snobbish]* Yes, I think I know the rules of the game, Mr. Allen.

Quinn: Then let's get started! Our first question is a math question, to test your knowledge.

Rudolph: Well, I am a human studies professor, but I'll do my best.

Quinn: Question: The circumference of a circle is determined by multiplying its diameter by what famous number?

Rudolph: I believe the answer is "pi."

Quinn: Very good, Professor, that's correct! *[Audience applauds as winning bell rings.]* Now audience, it's your turn to decide if Professor Primp made the wise decision. On the count of three, you know what to do: One, two, three!

Audience: Wise!

[Audience applauds and cheers.]

Quinn: That was a slam-dunk, Professor.

Rudolph: Thank you Quinn, it was nothing.

Quinn: Wisdom is more than just knowledge, so now we have a different kind of question to ask…

Rudolph: I can hardly wait.

Quinn: *[Holds up wallet, or points to it]* Here's a wallet that fell on the ground. We found it just moments ago. There isn't any I.D. in it, but it's full of cash. Professor, my question is: Would you keep this wallet or turn it in to the police?

Rudolph: Hmm, anyone smart enough to have a lot of money should be smart enough not to lose it. Since there's no way of knowing whose it is, it would appear that their loss is my gain. I'm going to keep the wallet.

Quinn: Is that your final answer?

Rudolph: Yes. I believe this will be a good lesson for whoever lost it, to help them remember not to lose something so valuable.

Quinn: Well that's certainly the choice many people would make, but is it wise? Let's ask the audience. One, two, three!

Audience: Not so wise!

Rudolph: *[Indignant]* Well, at least I answered the question honestly.

Quinn: That may be, Professor, but the fact of the matter is, the wallet isn't yours to keep. The wallet actually belongs to a tough construction worker named Wally who just got paid and needs the money to feed his family. Our producer was kind enough to tell him who found his wallet, and he just heard your answer. Oh! Here he comes right now!

Wally: *[Enters]* You were going to keep my money, huh?

Rudolph: I didn't know, um, it was yours.

Wally: Well you do now! Gimme that, you!

Rudolph: Oh, dear!

[Wally roughly takes the wallet from Rudolph. Rudolph follows as Wally exits. We hear scuffling, and then Rudolph re-enters.]

Quinn: You see, Professor, being smart and clever isn't the same as having wisdom. Wisdom comes from God, not from being intelligent.

Rudolph: Personally, I don't believe in God. He's just a fairy tale invented by kooky people to make them feel better about life.

Quinn: Professor, let's ask the audience what they think about that. One, two, three!

Audience: Not so wise!

Quinn: You see, Professor, even though you don't believe in God, He believes in you. One day you may understand that knowledge puffs you up like a big balloon full of hot air, but true wisdom builds you up. *[Begin music.]* Well, that's all the time we have for today. Be sure to ask yourself today, am I wise…or not so wise? *[Exits]*

Rudolph: Is that it? Did I win?

Wally: *[Enters]* There he is! That's the guy! Hey buddy, I want to talk to you! *[Wally chases Rudolph offstage.]*

Announcer: *[Offstage]* There you have it, boys and girls. Looks like using a little wisdom would have been a good idea for the good professor! Join us next time for the quiz show that tests your wits, *Wise or Not So Wise*.

[Fade music.]

LESSON 19

Detective Doodad and the Caged Convincer

1 Kings 18:20-39   Elijah and the Prophets of Baal

Focus: The world will lie to you to pull you away from the truth. But God is more powerful than anyone or anything. His truth will always triumph over evil.

Characters:

Detective Doodad: a brilliant yet eccentric detective who somehow always has the right answer.

Keona: a sensible and intelligent girl who likes to work things out.

Dr. D. Seaver: Detective Doodad's childhood friend and present-day archenemy, a master of disguise.

Props: Large cardboard rectangle with "bars" cut out of it (as jail cell door), small amount of flour or powder (for Dr. D. Seaver's "Denial Dust") and handkerchief.

The Setup: Techno City Jail.

[Begin music.]

Announcer: *[Offstage]* It's time again for the continuing adventures of Detective Doodad and the Doodad Gang! Today we find our hero questioning the recently captured Dr. D. Seaver. Detective Doodad has brought Keona along to try and help the mysterious doctor.

[Fade music. Detective Doodad and Keona enter on one side.]

Keona: I've never been inside a jail before.

Detective Doodad: That's a good thing, Keona. It's no fun to be locked up. But we're here to visit Dr. D. Seaver and maybe help him.

Keona: You want to help him?

Detective Doodad: Of course! But remember to stay alert for Dr. D. Seaver's lies. Don't believe what he says, because he'll do anything to escape.

Keona: OK!

Detective Doodad: Our God is more powerful than anything or anyone. His truth will help us overcome the enemy's lies.

[Detective Doodad and Keona walk to center stage. Dr. D. Seaver appears on the other side, behind bars. The door is between him and Keona.]

Dr. D. Seaver: Detective Doodad. Have you come to make fun of me?

Detective Doodad: No, Dr. D. Seaver. I just wanted to talk to you and see how you were doing.

Dr. D. Seaver: Talk? Talk about what, my favorite baseball team? You of all people should know how I'm doing. You put me here.

Keona: Don't blame us for your bad choices.

Dr. D. Seaver: Blame you? I don't blame you. But I will remember you!

Detective Doodad: Enough threats, Doctor. You have no power over us.

Keona: What happened to make you so full of hate?

Dr. D. Seaver: Why should I tell you? You'll just make fun of me.

Detective Doodad: No we won't. We're here to help. Tell us what happened, please.

Dr. D. Seaver: *[Falsely]* Oh, all right. It was many years ago, and it began on my seventh birthday.

Keona: Did you have a birthday cake?

Dr. D. Seaver: Yes, there was a cake, but more importantly, there was a wonderful gift.

Keona: What kind of gift?

Dr. D. Seaver: *[Stalling]* Oh, it was so many years ago, let me think. It was a, uh, a baseball!

Detective Doodad: A baseball made you evil?

Dr. D. Seaver: Let me finish! I loved the baseball, and I played with it every day, until someone stole it!

Keona: Who took it?

Dr. D. Seaver: A bully, and he wouldn't give it back. I tried and tried, but he was too big. So I began to plan my revenge. I'd get my baseball back, no matter what, and one day, I did!

Keona: Really? *[She gets closer.]* How'd you get it back?

Dr. D. Seaver: That's the delicious part. Come closer, and I'll tell you.

Keona: OK!

Detective Doodad: Not too close, Keona. Is this a true story, Dr. D. Seaver?

Dr. D. Seaver: Oh, absolutely. Why would I lie? I even have the baseball right here, in my hand. *[Holds hands behind back]* Would you like to see?

Keona: I would! *[Keona rushes over to see what's in Dr. D. Seaver's hand.]*

Detective Doodad: No Keona, stay back! It's a trick!

[There's a sound effect as a cloud of "Denial Dust" flies up from below the stage curtain into Keona's face.]

Dr. D. Seaver: Ha, ha, ha! A little Denial Dust will change her mind, Detective. She'll do whatever I say!

Keona: *[Dreamily]* What happened?

Dr. D. Seaver: You came to play ball with me, remember? Just open the door, and I'll come out.

Keona: *[Dazed]* All right. *[Reaches for the door]*

Detective Doodad: Keona, stop!

Keona: *[Dazed]* But Detective, I have to open the door.

Detective Doodad: He's trying to trick you, Keona. Don't be fooled! Dr. D. Seaver has no power over you unless you let him. Remember, God is more powerful than anything.

Dr. D. Seaver: Open the door!

Detective Doodad: Go, go, Doodad Hanky! *[He raises his hand with a handkerchief in it and goes to Keona.]* Sneeze, Keona, now!

Keona: *[Sneezing into the hanky]* Ah-choo!

Dr. D. Seaver: No! Don't listen to him!

Keona: *[Remembering]* Hey, you tried to trick me!

Dr. D. Seaver: Yes, but now you've messed up my whole plan.

Detective Doodad: That's our job, Dr. D. Seaver. Don't ever forget that God is more powerful than any of your evil plans.

Keona: Thank you for helping me remember the truth, Detective Doodad.

Detective Doodad: My pleasure, Keona. I'm glad you listened. Because if you play ball with evil, you're bound to strike out!

[Both exit, leaving Dr. D. Seaver *alone. Dr. D. Seaver* grunts and sulks. Begin music.*]*

Announcer: *[Offstage]* Once again, kids, good has triumphed over bad! That's because God is more powerful than anything or anyone—including the evil Dr. D! Thankfully, he's been captured, so things should settle down now for the Doodad Gang. Stay tuned until next time!

[Fade music.]

LESSON 21

Watch Out World, I'm Packing Praise!

2 Chronicles 20:2–26   Jehoshaphat's Great Victory

Focus: Are you singing the blues? Are you frustrated? Praise the Lord. Praising God is a powerful weapon for overcoming the problems of life. Next time you feel like screaming, praise the Lord instead.

Characters:
   Timmy: a boy who is having a bad day.
   King: Timmy's dog.
   Dad: Timmy's father.

Props: CD player and *The Next Generation Praise* CD cued to the song "Thank You Lord."

The Setup: Inside Timmy's house.

[Begin music. Timmy enters.]

Timmy: Mom! Dad! I'm home! Anybody here? *[Pause]* I can't believe this! It's the worst day of my life, and nobody's home.

[Timmy's dog, King, enters, barking.]

King: Woof! Woof!

Timmy: Hi, King. At least you're here.

King: Woof! *[King licks Timmy's face.]*

Timmy: *[Bothered]* King! You're licking me to death!

King: Woof, woof…WOOF!

Timmy: I'm not even going to try to stop you. I'm tired! Tired of school, tired of tests, I'm tired of the crummy weather, and I've had it! I think I'm going to officially retire from life.

King: Woof?

Timmy: What's this? It's another note from Dad. "Dear Timmy, I just ran down to the store to get some things for Mom. Please tackle the trash before you go upstairs. See you soon. Love, Dad."

King: Woof!

Timmy: That does it. This is definitely the worst day of my life. C'mon King, we'd better go get the trash out.

[Timmy starts to exit the stage. We hear a bump, a howl of pain, and Timmy falls out of view. He re-enters quickly, jumping up and down in pain.]

King: *[Alarmed]* Woof! Woof! Woof!

Timmy: *[Hopping up and down]* Ow! Ow! Oh, that hurts! Why did Mom have to buy the pointiest coffee table in the world? I always hit my knee on that corner…ow! Why do we even have a coffee table, anyway? The only things I ever see on it are Dad's feet!

[A door opens and closes. Dad enters the room and sees Timmy.]

Dad: Timmy? Are you hurt, son? Or is that the new skateboard move you're working on?

Timmy: No! It was the stupid table, Dad. It hit me right on my kneecap!

Dad: Well, sit down; let me take a look at it. King, you go sit down now, over there.

[King exits as Timmy stops hopping in place.]

Timmy: Did I break my leg?

Dad: No, but you bruised it pretty good. I think you'll live.

Timmy: That's not funny, Dad.

Dad: I'm kidding, Timmy. Why are you in such a bad mood?

Timmy: This has been the worst day of my life, Dad. I had a pop quiz at school; I lost my favorite baseball card; it rained all day so we couldn't play outside, and now this. What am I supposed to do when life throws me all these problems?

Dad: This may sound strange, Timmy, but the best thing to do when life gets bad is to fight back.

Timmy: How can I fight problems, Dad?

Dad: You fight problems by praising God.

Timmy: Praising God? How can that help?

Dad: Because praising the Lord is a powerful weapon to turn our bad days into good ones.

Timmy: That doesn't make any sense. Praise is a weapon?

Dad: Yes. When we praise God, we let go of our bad feelings and kick all of our problems up to God. You can't hit the rain with your fist, and it doesn't do any good to hit a door when you lose your favorite baseball card. But you can drive the devil away by praising God.

Timmy: God likes it when we praise Him, even if we're in a bad mood?

Dad: Especially when we're in a bad mood. Praise gives glory to God. In fact, it's hard to stay in a bad mood when you're singing God's praises.

Timmy: Really?

Dad: Yep. The next time you feel like screaming, Timmy, praise God instead. I guarantee it will make you feel better and help you deal with whatever happens.

Timmy: Wow, thanks Dad. I feel better already!

Dad: Good. Well, time for me to unload the car for your mom, OK? *[Exits]*

Timmy: OK, and I'll take the trash out! *[Timmy jumps up and hits the table again.]* Ow! Not again! *[Mad]* I want to take this table and…

[Timmy catches his breath, bows his head, and begins to sing, painfully at first.]

Timmy: "I come before you Lord, today…and there's just one thing that I want to say… thank You, Lord, thank You, Lord." Hey, this praise thing really does work. I feel better already.

[King enters, barking. Begin music, using "Thank You Lord" from The Next Generation Praise CD.]

King: Woof, woof!

Timmy: Hey, King, I'm singing praise to King Jesus! He's the King of kings! Watch out world, I'm packing praise!

[Timmy exits, singing. Fade music.]

Secrets for Puppet Ministry Success

Teaching the Basics

Many puppet teams struggle because they fail to place proper importance on learning the "basics" of puppet ministry technique. These include:

- Hand position in puppet's head
- Puppeteer body and arm positions
- Entering and exiting
- Eye contact, focus and positioning
- Appropriate and believable animation
- Correct lip synch
- Height of puppet with respect to stage
- Use of arm rods

As the director, provide feedback while the puppeteers practice their techniques. When clear, firm, encouraging and instructive feedback is given from week to week, you'll see great progress in skill development, plus positive attitudes from your team!

General Guidelines

Don't assume anything. Explain and demonstrate simple things like which hand to use, how to put the puppet on, hand position, arm position, and body position of the puppeteer.

Teach proper techniques. Make sure you have had proper training yourself, either in person or via video. Consider using a video or bring someone in to assist you in training your team. One Way Street, Inc. offers a "Reaching and Teaching" training video and a "Puppet Aerobics 2000" CD as useful training tools. (See ordering information on page 48.)

Stress proper body position. Demonstrate, then insist that everyone rehearse correctly. (Kneeling or standing position, no chairs, no arm crutches, no bent arms, knees or feet spread wide apart to provide balance, arm extended straight upward near ear, no sitting on heels, no slanted or distorted body angles.)

Provide height adjustment for shorter puppeteers. They will need kneeling pads, kneeling benches or something to stand or kneel on to get their puppets high enough to be seen. One Way Street, Inc. offers 2-inch-thick kneeling pads, so height can be adjusted depending upon the angle between the performance area and the audience. (See ordering information on page 48.)

How to Begin

Separate your rookies from the veterans. Your veterans need some drill and review to sharpen their puppetry techniques, but your new puppeteers need several weeks of concentrated training apart from the veterans. Another approach is to assign each rookie to a veteran, and spend a few rehearsals allowing the veteran to give one-on-one tutoring and feedback to the rookies.

Continued on page 48

LESSON 22

Detective Doodad and the Hostile Hearing

Esther 2:17; 4:14   Esther Saves Her People

Focus: God asks us to help our fellow Christians. He wants us to be encouraging and loyal to our brothers and sisters in Christ. That includes standing up for them when someone accuses them falsely. It's our job to be there for them in the tough times.

Characters:

Detective Doodad: a brilliant yet eccentric detective who somehow always has the right answer.
Henry: a younger boy who looks tough, but is gentle. Give him a computer, and he'll find your answer in no time.
Mindi Lee: the new girl in town. She's seemingly shy, but not afraid to fight for what's right.
Commissioner Slade: Police Commissioner. He is gruff, but fair.
Wiley Collins: Slade's assistant. He is deceptive and ambitious.

Props: Gavel, and microphone in the center of the stage.

The Setup: A courtroom. Commissioner Slade and Assistant Collins should be up on the second level of the stage, or off to one side.

[Begin music.]

Announcer: *[Offstage]* Time now for the continuing adventures of Detective Doodad and the Doodad Gang! This just in: bad news for Techno City! The evil Dr. D. Seaver has escaped from jail! Commissioner Slade has called a hearing to find out how this happened. Detective Doodad and the Doodad Gang will soon find themselves on the witness stand.

[Fade music. Slade *and* Collins *enter.]*

Slade: *[Bangs a gavel]* This hearing is now called to order. As you know, Dr. D. Seaver managed to escape from the Techno City jail two nights ago. Assistant Commissioner Wiley Collins will describe the events leading up to the escape.

Collins: Thank you, Commissioner Slade. Dr. D. Seaver escaped from his cell by drugging the prison guards. Then he used acid to burn a hole in the wall and escape. What we're trying to find out is if he had any outside help.

Slade: Mr. Collins, please call the first witness.

Collins: The commission calls Detective Doodad to the stand.

Detective Doodad: *[Enters]* Detective Doodad here! How can I help?

Slade: Detective, we're aware of your many years of service to the community. We just need to ask a few questions. How well did you know Dr. D. Seaver?

Detective Doodad: Better than I realized. We went to the same school as kids. But that was before he turned to a life of crime. I hardly recognized him as Dr. D. Seaver.

Collins: *[Accusing]* So, you've actually known this criminal since childhood?

Detective Doodad: Yes.

Collins: And you visited him many times in jail, Detective. Why was that?

Detective Doodad: Because I was trying to help him.

Slade: *[Surprised]* Help him do what, Detective?

Detective Doodad: To see the light and turn from his evil ways.

Collins: Why do you think Dr. D. Seaver came to Techno City in the first place? Didn't he visit you as soon as he arrived?

Detective Doodad: Well yes, but it wasn't a friendly visit. He tried to blow up my clubhouse!

Collins: Speaking of the clubhouse, I'd like to talk to some of your helpers.

Detective Doodad: They're right here. Henry, Mindi Lee? Please step up to the microphone.

[Henry and Mindi Lee enter.]

Slade: Now don't be afraid, children, just tell us what you know and be sure to tell the truth.

Collins: Henry, did you ever see Detective Doodad try to help Dr. D. Seaver?

Henry: Yes, sir, lots of times.

Collins: Did the Detective ever try to help Dr. D. Seaver escape?

Mindi Lee: No, it wasn't like that. Detective Doodad wants to help everybody, even someone as mean as Dr. D. Seaver.

Collins: But the fact is, Mindi Lee, every time the Doctor tried to escape, Detective Doodad had just visited him.

Henry: What does that have to do with anything?

Collins: I believe that Detective Doodad may have been helping Dr. D. Seaver all along. Helping him to escape! Detective Doodad is Dr. D. Seaver's partner in crime!

[Audience oohs and ahhs.]

Slade: *[Bangs gavel]* Order! Collins, that's quite an accusation!

Collins: Look at the evidence, Commissioner. They're old friends, Detective Doodad spent lots of time with him at the jail, and Dr. D. Seaver always manages to get away from the Doodad Gang at the last second. Isn't it obvious? The escape occurred right after a visit from the Detective.

Slade: Hmm. Detective, anything to say to these charges?

Mindi Lee: No wait, let me answer that. Dr. D. Seaver doesn't always get away. He wouldn't have been in jail if it wasn't for us, and we wouldn't have caught him if Detective Doodad hadn't trained us.

Slade: Go on, young lady.

Mindi Lee: Detective Doodad taught us to stand up for what's right, and now we're going to stand up for him.

Henry: Yeah! Detective Doodad is the good guy!

Mindi Lee: The Detective cares about everybody. He wants to see Dr. D. Seaver follow good, not evil. That's why he visited him so much, to show him that someone cared.

Collins: Detective Doodad is lying!

Mindi Lee: No, he's not. If you throw him in jail, you can throw all of us in jail. And then who will stop Dr. D. Seaver?

Slade: Hmm. *[Pauses]* Detective Doodad, this commission finds you innocent of all accusations. You've been a great helper in the fight against evil, and you have some very convincing friends. This court is adjourned! *[Bangs gavel]*

[Everyone exits. Begin music.]

Announcer: *[Offstage]* The Doodad Gang sure knows how to stand up for their leader, just as our Father God wants us to stand up for each other! Stay tuned for the continuing adventures of Detective Doodad and his loyal Doodad Gang!

[Fade music.]

Secrets for Puppet Ministry Success

Continued from page 45

Start with recorded songs and simple live puppetry. Try short, medium tempo puppet songs that consist of several voices singing together (no solos). Also try using live voices, saying Bible verses, counting or asking questions and having the puppet(eer) respond.

At first, use only one puppet arm-rod and let the arm hang when not in use. Practice natural arm movements, while learning lip synch, eye contact and other basic skills. After mastering the use of one rod, have your team practice with two.

Give lots of positive feedback as you correct technique. Go out of your way to make mention of the positive things you see happening. Warm, sincere, encouraging words will go a long way to soothe the aching arms and sore knees inherent in developing good puppetry technique.

Don't perform too soon. Beginner puppeteers need time to develop the arm strength, techniques and confidence that can only happen through at least five or six weeks of rehearsal.

Training new puppeteers is extremely important and requires a knowledgeable instructor, energetic and willing-to-learn puppeteers, sufficient time, privacy, patience and prayer.

Article, seventh in a series by Dale VonSeggen. "One Way Street News," April issue 2003. Reprinted with permission: One Way Street, Inc., P.O. Box 5077, Englewood, CO 80155, Phone: (303) 790-1188, Web site: www.onewaystreet.com

LESSON 23

What Were We Made to Do?

Psalm 63:1-8   Seeking God's Face in Worship

Focus: God created us with a purpose—to enjoy and to worship Him. We can spend our whole lives searching for why we're here, but the answer is clear: We were made to worship God.

Characters:

  Phil: A young boy.
  Jill: A young girl.

Props: Determine how many props or costumes you want to make for this rhyming script. Teams could choose to make every odd image and reference described, or to simply make a sign that says "We Were Made To Worship God." The more visual variety created, the more effective the script will be.

The Setup: Anywhere. Music plays throughout the entire script. The rhyme is set to the beat of the song "You're Worthy Of My Praise" from *The Next Generation Praise* CD. The tempo of the song is fairly fast, so the rhyme will sound like a rap at times.

[Begin music. Phil and Jill enter, moving to the beat.]

Jill: *[Rhyming]* Hello Phil, it's a lovely day. *[Pause for four beats of the music.]*

Phil: Hello Jill, let's run and play. *[Pause for four beats.]*

Jill: Let's run and play and dance and sing. *[Pause for four beats.]*

Phil: I think there's time for everything. *[Pause for four beats.]*

Jill: What will we play; what will we do?

Phil: I have an answer game for you.

Jill: An answer game? How do we play?

Phil: We answer what I ask today. Here's the question, answer, please: *[Pause for four beats.]* Why did God make you and me?

[Pause for four beats as Jill thinks. Increase music volume.]

Jill: God made me special, this I know,
I think I could learn to sew
I could sew on butterfly wings
Flower petals and pretty things

I could make a pair of pants
So big they'd hold a million ants!
Knit a sweater, soft and warm
To keep me dry in thunderstorms.

If I sew it's not too odd
I was made to worship God. *[Pause for four beats.]*

Phil: Pants for ants and thunder sweaters
Maybe I'll tell 'bout stormy weather
Fly up in the clouds so high
Catch a raindrop in my eye

Twist and turn like a tornado
Red sunburn like a tomato
Winter chill to frost my nose
White snowflakes and toasty clothes

Yet rain or snow or lightning rod
I was made to worship God. *[Pause for four beats.]*

Jill: Even if I glow so bright
Like a firefly in the night
Bright and shiny, large or small
Spreading light for one and all.

I could light the way for planes
Be a spotlight for cars and trains
Biggest light bulb in the world
Shining out to boys and girls.

A light upon the path I trod
I was made to worship God! *[Pause for four beats.]*

Phil: Maybe I was meant to grow
To spread my roots like plants you know
Sink my feet deep in the ground
And soak up water all around.

I'd lift my branch and grow some leaves
Knobby knots to scare off thieves
Make some fruit, perhaps some melons
Some to give, and some for sellin'

Like a flower in the sod
I was made to worship God. *[Pause for four beats.]*

Jill: I like this game; I like to play. *[Pause for four beats.]*

Phil: It's easy to get carried away. We can do all kinds of things; our purpose is to praise the King!

Jill: I can worship down the hall
In my bed, or at the mall.

Phil: I can worship while I sing
Fly a kite, or pull some string.

Jill: Even if I'm tall or skinny
Rich or poor, without a penny.

Phil: I can worship all my days
In a fog or in a haze.

Jill: God made me to worship Him
Even if I'm thick or thin
On the land or in a boat
I will let His praises float.

Phil: Underground, in outer space
I will learn to seek His face
Wearing blue or wearing yellow
I will be a joyful fellow.

Both: *[Together]* We're just like peas in a pod
We were made to worship God!

Jill: You don't need a worship team
A fishing pole or lima beans
You don't even need a reason
Worship is for any season.

Phil: *[To audience]* Now you know why we were made
Lift your voice and give us aid
Sing out loud and join the squad
"I was made to worship God."

Jill: I was made to worship God.

Both: We were made to worship God!

[Crescendo music, then end. Phil *and* Jill *exit.]*

LESSON 25

The Doodad Gang on the Hunt

Isaiah 6:1–8   Isaiah's Call

Focus: Each one of us has a job to do for God. He calls us to go where He needs us to do His work. It's up to us to listen and go where He sends us.

Characters:

Detective Doodad: a brilliant yet eccentric detective who somehow always has the right answer.
Henry: a younger boy who looks tough, but is gentle. Give him a computer, and he'll find your answer in no time.
Keona: a sensible and intelligent girl who likes to work things out.
Tony: a natural leader who tends to jump in with both feet.
Mindi Lee: the new girl in town. She's seemingly shy, but not afraid to fight for what's right.

Props: Radio prop with an antenna (or old laptop, visible to the audience).

The Setup: The Doodad Gang clubhouse.

[Begin music.]

Announcer: *[Offstage]* It's time once again for the continuing adventures of Detective Doodad and the Doodad Gang. Detective Doodad is on the hunt for the elusive Dr. D. Seaver, who's been spotted in Techno City. The Doodad Gang has fanned out across town, except for Henry, who's stayed behind to monitor communications.

[Fade music. Detective Doodad and Henry enter.]

Detective Doodad: Henry, the rest of the gang is out looking for clues so we can find Dr. D. Seaver. I need you to stay here at the radio and answer any questions they might have when they call in.

Henry: Sure, Detective Doodad. I can do that.

Detective Doodad: If I call for you, leave here and come immediately. No matter what, remember this: You need to go wherever I send you.

Henry: Yes, sir.

Detective Doodad: I'm sure you'll do a great job, Henry. We'll catch Dr. D. Seaver! *[Exits]*

Henry: Wow, I'm in charge of communications for the whole Doodad Gang. This is cool!

[Keona enters on another level of the stage, preferably the upper level. She talks into her wrist communicator.]

Keona: Keona to base; come in base.

Henry: I'm here, Keona. How can I help you?

Keona: Henry, I need to know if Tony's in Sector 5 yet.

Henry: Roger, Keona, I'll find out for you.

Keona: Have Tony call me directly. Thanks Henry! *[Exits]*

Henry: No problem, Keona. Base to Tony; come in Tony.

[Tony enters on another upper level of the stage.]

Tony: *[Talking into wrist]* Hey, radioman! How's it going?

Henry: Just fine, Tony. Are you in Sector 5 yet?

Tony: Yeah, I just got here. No sign of Dr. D. Seaver anywhere.

Henry: Great. Please call Keona and let her know exactly where you are, OK?

Tony: Okay. Tony out! *[Exits]*

Henry: Man, this is awesome. I can talk to everyone from here. But I have to go if the Detective calls for me. That's the important thing.

[Mindi Lee enters on upper level of the stage.]

Mindi Lee: *[Talking into wrist]* Henry, this is Mindi Lee. Are you there?

Henry: Yes, Mindi Lee, I'm here. What do you need?

Mindi Lee: The Detective found a clue, and he thinks Dr. D. Seaver is headed toward Sector 5. He wanted you to text message the police and let them know.

Henry: No problem, Mindi Lee. I'm on it. *[Keyboard sounds as he types]*

Mindi Lee: Thanks, Henry! Mindi Lee out. *[Exits]*

Henry: Go, go, Doodad fingers! Text message is done!

[Detective Doodad appears where Tony was. He speaks into the wrist communicator.]

Detective Doodad: Detective Doodad to Henry, come in Henry.

Henry: Yes, Detective, I hear you.

Detective Doodad: Dr. D. Seaver has been spotted in Sector 5. I think he's trying to slip between Tony and Keona. I need you to go to Sector 5 right now.

Henry: Yes, sir, I understand!

Detective Doodad: Good. You'll meet the police there, and search the area. I'm on my way. Detective Doodad out! *[Exits]*

Henry: Wow, Detective Doodad wants me to go out and help. There's no time to waste.

[Dr. D. Seaver appears in an upper corner of the stage. He disguises his voice to sound like Detective Doodad.]

Dr. D. Seaver: Uh, hello, testing, Detective Doodad here!

Henry: Yes Detective, it's Henry. You sound funny.

Dr. D. Seaver: Trust me, I'm not funny.

[Pause as Dr. D. Seaver *slides to one side.]* Can you hear me now?

Henry: *[Pause]* Yes, that's better.

Dr. D. Seaver: I'm calling to tell you to stay right where you are. Don't do anything.

Henry: But Detective, you just told me to go to Sector 5.

Dr. D. Seaver: Whatever you do, don't go to Sector 5! In fact, maintain radio silence. Don't talk to anyone, Henry. That's an order. Obey me, or else! *[Exits]*

Henry: Hmmm. That was weird. Detective Doodad told me to go, but now I hear his voice saying don't go. What do I do? I think I need to ask God. *[Prays]* Lord, I need Your help. Please show me the right way to go. Amen. *[Remembering]* Hey! Detective Doodad said no matter what, I needed to go if he called me. And he did call me. I'm going to go where he sent me. Sector 5, here I come!

[Henry exits. Begin music.]

Announcer: *[Offstage]* Tune in next time for the continuing adventures of Detective Doodad and the Doodad Gang, when we discover just what happens when we go where God wants us to go!

[Fade music.]

LESSON 26

Detective Doodad and the Opulent Offer

Ezekiel 37:1–14   Ezekiel and the Dry Bones

Focus: Our God is the great Creator, the One who made us and the One who gives us new life in His Son, Christ Jesus. He has made us His children and given us His Spirit to comfort us, guide us and renew our hearts and minds. God's Spirit gives us new life.

Characters:

Detective Doodad: a brilliant yet eccentric detective who somehow always has the right answer.

Tony: a natural leader who tends to jump in with both feet.

Dr. D. Seaver: Detective Doodad's childhood friend and present-day archenemy, a master of disguise.

Keona: a sensible and intelligent girl who likes to work things out.

Props: Laser pointer and flashlight.

The Setup: An old mill near a river. Dim the lights or have dim stage lighting during this skit. The phrase "Uh-oh. That's not good" is repeated throughout the skit. Play up the phrase throughout. For added humor, have the characters say it the same way each time.

[Begin music.]

Announcer: *[Offstage]* Welcome again to the adventures of Detective Doodad and the Doodad Gang! Good news: The Doodad Gang has cornered the evil Dr. D. Seaver in an old mill outside the city. Detective Doodad and Tony are searching the building while the rest of the Doodad Gang watch the exits and wait for the police to arrive.

[Fade music. Detective Doodad and Tony enter. Lights up.]

Detective Doodad: Stay close, Tony. There's no telling where Dr. D. Seaver could be hiding.

Tony: *[Looking around and whispering]* How are we going to find him, Detective? He's a master of disguise.

Detective Doodad: Dr. D. Seaver has a lot of tricks up his sleeve, but none of them are new. He likes the darkness. But we're walking in the light.

Tony: Yeah, it's a good thing the lights are still on in this old mill. *[Lights go out.]* Uh-oh. That's not good.

Detective Doodad: Looks like the Doctor is trying to make things a little more difficult for us. Go, go, Doodad Laser Pointer! *[Detective Doodad raises his arm and waves the laser pointer around as the lights fade up to dim.]* This little light of mine, I'm going to let it shine!

Tony: Hey, now that's good! I can let my light shine, too. *[Tony raises a flashlight and shines it around.]*

Detective Doodad: Dr. D. Seaver, I know you're in here. There's no use in trying to escape. Let us help you.

Dr. D. Seaver: *[Offstage]* Help me, Detective? Of course you can help me—by letting me sneak out the back.

Tony: Uh-oh. That's not good.

Detective Doodad: *[Looking all around]* I can't do that, Dr. D. Seaver. Besides, you'll never escape from a life of crime until you give up.

Tony: The whole building's surrounded anyway.

Detective Doodad: Tony's right, Dr. D. Seaver. Your only hope is to make the right choice and turn yourself in.

Dr. D. Seaver: *[His head appears on the upper level, above Detective Doodad and Tony.]* Hope? There's no hope for me, Detective Doodad. *[Exits]*

Tony: There's always hope!

Detective Doodad: Dr. D. Seaver, you need to give up doing things your own way, and stop making bad choices.

Dr. D. Seaver: *[His head pops up in a different place.]* How can I stop making bad choices, when that's all I ever had? I'm bad because my whole life has been bad. That's all God has ever given me. *[Exits]*

Detective Doodad: *[Still searching]* God wasn't the one who brought bad things into your life. You've been deceived, Dr. D. Seaver. God wants to give you a new life.

Tony: *[Looking around and whispering]* Detective Doodad, I think Dr. D. Seaver is trying to sneak out the back and reach the river.

Detective Doodad: *[Quietly]* Uh-oh. That's not good. If he gets into the river, we'll never catch him. I know! *[Talks into wrist]* Detective Doodad to Keona.

Keona: *[Offstage]* I'm here, Detective. How's it going?

Detective Doodad: Dr. D. Seaver turned off the lights. It's pitch black in here.

Keona: Uh-oh. That's not good.

Detective Doodad: I'm sending Tony out to help. I need you two to find the power switch and turn the lights back on.

Keona: *[Offstage]* OK, Detective!

Detective Doodad: *[To Tony]* Move quietly, Tony. Don't let the Doctor hear you.

Tony: Yes, sir! *[Tony exits.]*

[Flicker lights, then fade.]

Detective Doodad: Uh-oh. That's not good. My laser pointer's battery is dying. I have to find Dr. D. Seaver now.

Dr. D. Seaver: *[Enters on the same level as Detective Doodad]* Well, well, well, it looks like I found you first. Is your lamp burning low, Detective? Uh, oh. That's not good! Ha, ha, ha, ha.

Detective Doodad: Never mind the hardware, Dr. D. Seaver. Are you going to change, or keep going your own way?

Dr. D. Seaver: It's too late for me to change, Detective.

Detective Doodad: It's never too late for God to change you. All you have to do is say yes to Him. It's the best offer in the world. What do you say? *[Turn lights completely out. There's a splash. Turn lights on.]* Dr. D. Seaver? Are you still here?

[Tony and Keona run in.]

Tony: Detective Doodad!

Keona: Are you OK?

Detective Doodad: *[Sadly]* Yes, I'm fine. But Dr. D. Seaver isn't. He's gone again. And he won't change. He'll never have a new life until he gives his life to God.

[Detective Doodad, Keona and Tony exit. Begin music.]

Announcer: *[Offstage]* That's it for today, kids, as Detective Doodad and the Doodad Gang continue to reach out to the dark-hearted Dr. D. Seaver.

[Fade music.]

LESSON 29

The Town Where Every Child Rides

Habakkuk 2:2-4   The Vision of Habakkuk

Focus: God has a purpose for your life, and the dreams you have are fulfilled in following His plan. Run with the ideas God gives you. He will help you make them come true.

Characters:

The Narrator
Harry Beam: a little boy with a big idea.
Cornelius Pratt: a wealthy businessman.
Two sad kids (one with red hair)
Two or three classmates
Policeman

Props: Red bicycle prop, bicycle parts, two additional bicycle props and big check. (The more props and visuals, the better.)

The Setup: Harry's town. Music plays throughout.

[Begin music. Harry enters.]

Narrator: *[Offstage]*
This is the story of Harry Beam
A little boy with a very big dream
He liked helping others; really, it's true
So God gave Harry an idea or two.

[Harry fixes things.]
Harry was good with his hands and his mind
He could fix anything broken he'd find
Toasters or coasters or busted up locks
Harry could fix it, quick as a fox.

[Red bicycle prop appears.]
He was so handy he built his own bike
A gorgeous contraption that everyone liked
With red handlebars and chrome all over
Harry would ride it from Dalton to Dover.

[Sad children enter. Narrator does the children's voices when they "speak."]
Riding one day through the town of Leaping,
Harry saw some children were weeping
He asked them, "Tell me, what is the matter?"
What they told Harry left him much sadder.

"We have no bicycles," one boy said
"No bikes to ride," piped a little redhead
"So we walk, or run, or play in the street
A bike of our own would really be neat.

We like your bicycle, Harry we do
All of us wish we could ride just like you
Maybe one day we'll learn how to pedal
Our own bikes made out of rubber and metal."

[Sad children exit.]
Harry rode home without saying a word
Deep in his heart something quiet had stirred
A plan took shape in his wonderful mind
A plan to help others, both thoughtful and kind

[Classmates enter.]
Monday at school Harry did something funny
He asked his friends for their time and their money
They thought he was joking like kids often do
When he kept asking they soon became rude.

"We won't give you money for some silly dream
If you keep asking we're going to get steamed
We won't give you any of our busy time

We won't give you money, not even a dime!"

[Classmates *exit.*]

Harry was sad, but his purpose was clear
He didn't give in to the doubts or the fears
He started collecting old bicycle parts
And then went to work with a joy in his heart

[Bicycle parts *appear.*]

Harry Beam's father soon noticed the clutter
When searching one day for his favorite putter
When asked, Harry told him, "It's part of my plot
To give needy children the bikes they ain't got."

Harry's father was touched to the core
Quickly he helped his son gather some more
They dove in the dumpster and picked through the junkyard
Finding old bike parts was not very hard.

[Bike parts *exit,* two bicycles *appear.* Sad children *re-enter.*]

Pretty soon Harry had built two nice bikes
He rode back to Leaping and found those small tikes
With a smile on his face he presented the prize
And laughed when he saw all the joy in their eyes.

[Children *exit with bicycles.*]

Harry went looking for others in need
He rebuilt and repaired old bikes with great speed
Word soon got out of his generous acts
One day a policeman stopped by for the facts.

[Policeman *enters.*]

Harry began to describe what he'd done
The officer sat there and listened, quite stunned
When Harry had finished the officer sat
He picked up his radio and took off his hat.

The officer called his friends on the force
He asked for their help, which they offered, of course
They'd bring old bicycles to Harry's house
He'd fix them and then they'd help him give them out.

[Policeman *exits.*]

Soon the newspaper caught wind of the scheme
And published a story about Harry's dream
To give needy children some bikes of their own
Before Harry knew it, his story had grown.

[Pratt *enters.*]

It caught the attention of Cornelius Pratt
A wealthy inventor of this and of that
Cornelius visited Harry one day
And said to him, "Young man, I've something to say."

Your dream is a worthy one, I will confide
I, too, was a child who had no bike to ride
The joy you bring is a gift that you share
It's nice to meet someone who's willing to care.

I'd like to ensure that your work doesn't end
Please accept this large check from me as a friend
You can buy all the bicycle parts you can find
And I'm also giving you a garage that was mine."

[Pratt *hands* Harry *big check and exits.*]

Harry thanked Pratt for his help and his aid
But most of all Harry thanked God every day
For God gave a young man the vision inside
To help build a town where every child rides.

[Harry *exits. Fade music.*]

LESSON 30

The Doodad Gang and the Powerful Presence

Haggai 1:2–2:9   Haggai and the New Temple

Focus: God's presence lives in us; our bodies, our hearts and our minds are His temple. He is with us wherever we go, and His Spirit helps us to go His way. In everything we do, we need to trust Him as our source.

Characters:

Detective Doodad: a brilliant yet eccentric detective who somehow always has the right answer.
Tony: a natural leader who tends to jump in with both feet.
Keona: a sensible and intelligent girl who likes to work things out.
Henry: a younger boy who looks tough, but is gentle. Give him a computer, and he'll find your answer in no time.
Mindi Lee: the new girl in town. She's seemingly shy, but not afraid to fight for what's right.

Props: Whistle and sheet of paper.

The Setup: Doodad Gang clubhouse.

[Begin music.]

Announcer: *[Offstage]* Time now for the continuing story of Detective Doodad and the Doodad Gang! After their close encounter with Dr. D. Seaver, the Doodad Gang is regrouping for their next mission. Detective Doodad is about to leave for a meeting at City Hall, but before he does, he has a few words for the Doodad Gang.

[Fade music. Detective Doodad, Henry, Mindi Lee and Keona enter.]

Detective Doodad: I have to go to this meeting, everyone, but at least we've had a few days of rest.

Mindi Lee: Rest is good, but we have a lot of work to do, Detective.

Keona: Yeah, a bunch of our equipment needs upgrading. We need new software, new hardware and new "every-ware!"

Detective Doodad: You're right, Keona. But don't forget, everyone: No matter how much work there is, our strength doesn't come from getting things done. The Lord is working in all of us, and it's His presence that keeps us going. *[Exits]*

Henry: Do you think Dr. D. Seaver will try to attack here again?

Keona: Dr. D. Seaver is always looking for ways to stop us, Henry. But never fear; God is here.

Henry: Yeah. He'll help us, no matter what happens.

Mindi Lee: Even Dr. D. Seaver can't take that away.

Keona: So where should we begin?

Mindi Lee: I'm going to start by cleaning the wrist communicators.

Henry: Good idea, Mindi Lee. I'll help you.

Keona: Speaking of work, where's Tony?

Henry: He said he was going to make up a list of things to do.

Keona: A list? Why do we need a list?

[Tony enters excitedly, blowing a whistle and waving a list.]

Tony: Because there's not a moment to lose, people! We've got a lot of work to do. Stuff to fix, things to build. It's all right here on the list!

Henry: The list?

Tony: To keep us on the right track, Henry. This list spells out exactly what we have to do, and exactly when we have to do it. C'mon, we're already past our time for talking.

Keona: Wait a second, Tony. How did you come up with this list?

Tony: Easy! I used my super huge brainpower to write down everything we need to do, from the most important to the least important.

Mindi Lee: *[Rolling her eyes]* Oh, brother!

Keona: And how are we ever going to get all this done?

Tony: I thought you'd never ask. I'll use my most excellent skills as a natural leader to make sure we don't miss anything.

Keona: I hate to be the one to tell you, Tony, but you've already missed something.

Tony: What? No I didn't. I've covered everything!

Henry: You missed the most important thing of all, Tony.

Tony: Oh, yeah. Item 34: ORDER PIZZA.

Mindi Lee: No, not pizza! You left out God.

Tony: God? *[Looks at list]* Oh, yeah, OK. If I shave off 10 minutes from lunch, we might be able to squeeze in a prayer and a chorus. Done. Let's move, people!

Keona: You've got this all backwards, Tony. God's not some little item on our list; He's the whole reason we have a list!

Henry: Yeah! Whatever we do, we do for Him. And the cool thing is, wherever we go, He's always with us, giving us the strength.

Tony: So I need to make up a new list?

Keona: Your list is fine, Tony, but don't forget that the Lord is the One who lives on the inside of us. He shows us what to do and might even make some changes on the lists we make.

Mindi Lee: God's presence in us gives us life. And He's always there for us.

Henry: If we forget about Jesus, none of this means a thing. He's the power source.

Tony: *[Understanding]* I think I get it now. I guess I got so caught up in what needs to be done that I forgot to depend on Him.

Keona: Maybe the first thing on our list should be praising God for giving us the strength to face whatever comes.

Tony: And asking Him what He wants us to do.

Mindi Lee: Now that's the way to start the day!

[Everyone exits. Begin music.]

Announcer: *[Offstage]* Looks like the Doodad Gang has figured out where their strength really comes from! Kids, with God's presence in our lives, we'll all have the power and guidance we need to do what He wants us to do! See you next time for the continuing adventures of Detective Doodad and the Doodad Gang!

[Fade music.]

Easy Seven-step Puppet Stage

Here's a quick and easy way to create your own puppet stage. It won't cost a lot of money, will be sturdier than PVC pipe and can be built in a day!

Materials Needed:

- measuring tape
- electric drill and bits
- electric saw
- electric staple gun and staples
- scissors (or X-acto knife)
- 12 2½-inch wood screws per panel
- Diagram of framework for panels
- glue mixed with warm water
- two-by-twos, cut to desired length (2 sides, top, middle and bottom per panel)
- paint primer
- black paint
- colored paint
- nuts and bolts (2 per panel)
- bucket
- canvas

1) Measure the area you've designated for your stage, then head to the lumberyard to purchase some two-by-twos.
2) Screw boards together to make rectangular frames for the panels you will cover and connect (see diagram using 5-foot tall panels).
3) Pre-drill holes for nuts and bolts to connect the panels (6 inches from top and bottom of each panel).
4) Soak canvas in bucket of glue and warm water.
5) Stretch canvas across wooden framework and staple it to the back of the boards on all four sides. (Do this for every panel.) Cut holes in canvas where connecting bolts will go.
6) Paint canvas sides with primer; then paint whatever scenery is desired.
7) Connect sides with nuts and bolts, and your puppet stage is ready for action! (See illustration.)

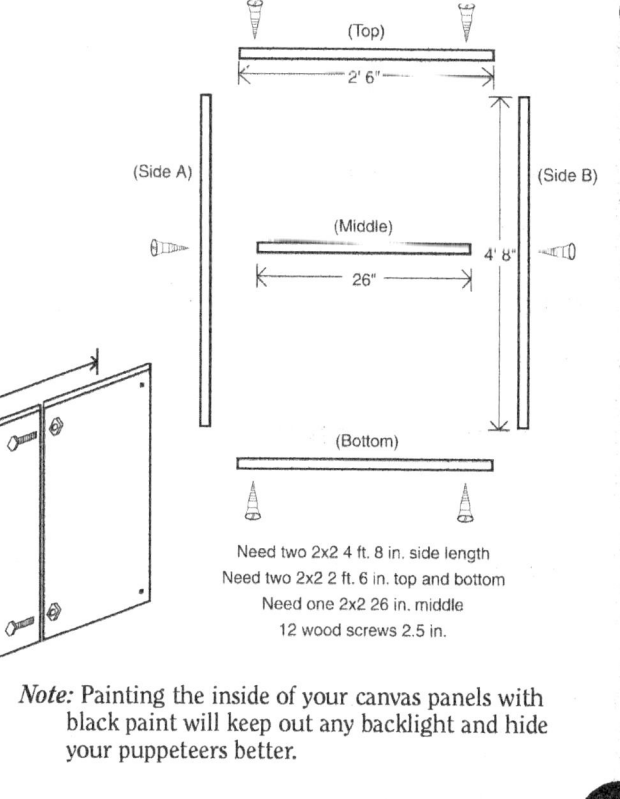

Need two 2x2 4 ft. 8 in. side length
Need two 2x2 2 ft. 6 in. top and bottom
Need one 2x2 26 in. middle
12 wood screws 2.5 in.

Note: Painting the inside of your canvas panels with black paint will keep out any backlight and hide your puppeteers better.

LESSON 32

Detective Doodad and the Anti-Attitude Attack

Matthew 5:1–12   The Beatitudes

Focus: Your inner thoughts affect how you act. You can choose to have a bad attitude or a good attitude. Though it's sometimes difficult to make the choice for good, God's blessing always results from a good attitude.

Characters:

Detective Doodad: a brilliant yet eccentric detective who somehow always has the right answer.
Tony: a natural leader who tends to jump in with both feet.
Mindi Lee: the new girl in town. She's seemingly shy, but not afraid to fight for what's right.
Dr. D. Seaver: Detective Doodad's childhood friend and present-day archenemy, a master of disguise.

The Setup: A ballpark.

[Begin music.]

Announcer: *[Offstage]* Welcome again to the adventures of Detective Doodad and the Doodad Gang! *[Sings]* Take me out to the ballgame! That's the tune the Doodad Gang is singing today as they take a break to watch a game of baseball. Little do they realize that Dr. D. Seaver has also come to the ballpark, and he's up to no good.

[Fade music. Detective Doodad, Henry and Keona enter.]

Henry: Thanks for the great seats, Detective Doodad!

Detective Doodad: You're welcome, Henry.

Keona: What team are the Techno City Techs playing today?

Henry: The Baymont Bombers. This is going to be a great game, Keona! We might even catch a fly ball!

Detective Doodad: That's the spirit! I'm glad to see you have a great attitude. I can tell you remember what I taught you back at the clubhouse.

Henry: *[Reciting from memory]* "I'm blessed when I have a good attitude." That's a totally cool idea.

Keona: God wants everyone to know that I have the joy of the Lord on my face like I do in my heart.

Detective Doodad: Right! The game's about to begin. Has anyone seen Tony or Mindi Lee?

Henry: They should have been here already.

Detective Doodad: They're probably just waiting in line. In the meantime, whoever wants a hot dog better follow me!

[Detective Doodad, Henry, and Keona exit. Tony and Mindi Lee enter on the second level.]

Tony: Hey, these seats aren't next to the field.

Mindi Lee: Yeah, they're almost behind the big TV screen.

Tony: You're right. We wouldn't see much from here.

Mindi Lee: It sure was fun climbing the stairs, though.

Tony: Let's go ask that usher if we're in the right place. I'll race you!

Mindi Lee: OK!

[Tony *and* Mindi Lee *exit.* Dr. D. Seaver *appears where they were.*]

Dr. D. Seaver: Oh, you're in the right place, my little Doodad friends. Once I play my "Anti-Attitude" video on the stadium screen, everyone will be hypnotized into a very bad mood. Then, while they're busy fighting with each other, I'll have time to rob the ticket office. Ha, ha, ha, ha. *[Exits]*

[Tony *and* Mindi Lee *re-enter.*]

Tony: He was right here. Where did he go?

Mindi Lee: Hey, look up there, behind the screen.

Tony: That's him. He's talking into a microphone.

[Dr. D. Seaver *appears above them.*]

Dr. D. Seaver: Ladies and gentlemen, please direct your attention to the big screen for a very important announcement. Keep your eyes on the screen at all times!

[*A hypnotic sound effect begins.* Tony *and* Mindi Lee *look around.*]

Tony: What in the world? Look at the crowd, Mindi Lee. They look hypnotized!

Mindi Lee: They are hypnotized. It's the video screen, Tony! Don't look at it!

Tony: I just want a quick peek!

[Tony *stares up at the screen.*]

Dr. D. Seaver: Well, if it isn't the Doodad Gang!

Mindi Lee: Dr. D. Seaver!

Dr. D. Seaver: How do you like my little video? Go ahead, take a peek.

Mindi Lee: No, I won't look.

Dr. D. Seaver: Oh come now, you'll feel so much worse if you do, just like your friend.

Tony: *[In a trance]* I hate baseball; I hate crowds! I'm going to bite someone's head off! *[Angrily directed at* Mindi Lee*]* Starting with you.

Mindi Lee: Tony, it's me, Mindi Lee. Don't forget what the Detective taught us: I am blessed when I have a good attitude; I am blessed when I have a good attitude.

Dr. D. Seaver: Stop saying that! You'll break my trance.

Tony: *[Groggily]* Mindi Lee? Is that you?

Mindi Lee: I'm right here, Tony. You were under Dr. D's spell.

Dr. D. Seaver: I'd love to stay and chat, but I have a ticket office to rob.

Detective Doodad: *[Enters]* Oh no you don't, Dr. D. Seaver.

Dr. D. Seaver: *[Surprised]* Detective Doodad! How did you know?

Detective Doodad: One quick look at that video and I knew you were behind it.

Dr. D. Seaver: You're always messing up my plans and leaving me in a bad mood! I'll be back to get you for this! *[Exits]*

Tony: Detective, he's getting away!

Detective Doodad: The police are here. I'm more concerned about you. Are you all right, Tony?

Tony: Yeah. Mindi Lee reminded me that I am blessed when I have a good attitude. By changing my attitude, I broke Dr. D. Seaver's hold over me.

Detective Doodad: God will always make a way for us to break the enemy's power. Come on, let's go find the others.

[Detective Doodad, Tony, and Mindi Lee exit. Begin music.]

Announcer: *[Offstage]* Tony discovered the power of a good attitude and helped foil the plans of the evil Dr. D. Seaver—the only one left with an attitude problem! Will Dr. D. Seaver escape the police once more? Will the Doodad Gang have another encounter with their archenemy? Will the baseball game ever get started? Tune in next time, for the continuing story…

[Fade music.]

LESSON 33

The Ultimate Calling Plan

Matthew 6:9–15   The Lord's Prayer

Focus: Prayer is the way we talk and listen to God— anytime, anywhere. Prayer keeps us connected with our heavenly Father, just like talking to our best friends keeps us close to them. Prayer builds friendship with God.

Characters:

Narrator: an offstage voice or adult man.
Dana: girl with a cell phone.
Cami: Dana's best friend, who also has a phone.

Props: Two cell phone props (one for Dana and one for Cami).

The Setup: A neighborhood.

[Begin music. Narrator and Dana enter.]

Narrator: Hi, kids, I'm your handy dandy Narrator. You know—the guy who explains the story. And this is the story of Dana, a young girl, just like some of you.

Dana: Hi everybody, I'm Dana!

Narrator: Dana lives in a neighborhood, just like some of you.

Dana: *[Pointing]* This is my neighborhood. My house is right there, across the street. My school is two blocks that way, next to the post office. And down there is the shopping mall, where Mom and I go to look for all kinds of cool stuff...

Narrator: As you may have noticed, Dana is good at making conversation.

Dana: I'm good at what?

Narrator: You're good at making conversation; that means you like to talk.

Dana: Oh yes, I love to talk! Especially to my best friend, Cami! She's so cool!

Narrator: Dana and Cami do love to talk. That's what best friends do. If you can't talk to your best friend, who else can you talk to?

Dana: I have so got to tell Cami I'm talking to a Narrator.

[Dana lifts her phone and dials. Cami enters on another level with a phone to her ear.]

Cami: Hi, this is Cami.

Dana: Cami!

Cami: Dana! How's it going?

Dana: Way cool, how are you?

Narrator: Like I said, they love to talk.

Cami: Like, who is that guy talking?

Dana: That's why I was calling you, to tell you I'm talking to the Narrator.

Cami: No way! You are, you really are?

Dana: Yes, I am.

Cami: That's so cool. What's a Narrator?

Dana: I don't know, I think he's a pilot or something. Oh, but never mind that, did I tell you what happened to me last night?

Cami: Before or after I called?

Dana: After.

Cami: No! What happened? Tell me everything!

Narrator: Dana and Cami tell each other about everything; they talk about clothes, school, families—especially little brothers who keep sneaking into their rooms and messing with their stuff.

Cami: No doubt! You will not believe what Riley did to my room last week!

Dana: Oh, yes I would. What happened? *[Both girls exit, talking.]*

Narrator: Even though they're miles apart, the girls are closer than sisters through the wonder of technology. And they talk on their phones wherever they are: at home, at school, at the store, inside, outside, rain or shine, Dana and Cami stay close to each other.

[Dana and Cami re-enter on different levels, talking on their phones.] One day, the girls were on their phones, talking, as usual.

Dana: Cami! You absolutely have to meet me at the mall. The boutique has the new fall collection in!

Cami: Ooooh! We can eat lunch together, and I can tell you all about that groovy concert I just went to.

Dana: Sounds like a plan. Oh! And I have the best new song to play for you!

Narrator: Suddenly, the line went dead; their phones had lost service.

Cami: Dana? Dana! Are you there?

Dana: Cami! I can't hear you!

Narrator: The conversation was over. They tried to call each other back, but the worst had happened: Dana and Cami had been disconnected!

Dana and Cami: *[Screaming]* Aaaaagh!

Dana: Oh, no! What am I going to do? I have plenty of battery left. Think, Dana, think!

Cami: *[Struggling]* Must…stay…calm. Must… get…to…mall! *[Exits]*

Dana: Cami knows to meet me at the mall. I'll head there right now. *[Exits]*

Narrator: Dana and Cami were such good friends, they knew they hadn't hung up on each other. They were close, and they couldn't wait to talk to each other once again.

[Dana and Cami enter on the same level and meet in the middle.]

Cami: *[Sees Dana]* Dana!

Dana: Cami!

Cami: I couldn't hear you!

Dana: We were disconnected.

Cami: I know! I'm so glad we're together again. Let's eat!

[Begin music.]

Narrator: *[Offstage]* Dana and Cami walked and talked all afternoon. They were the best of friends. *[Dana and Cami hug, and exit.]* We also have a friend who we can talk to anytime, anywhere. His name is Jesus. We don't need cell phones or e-mail to talk to Jesus. We can talk to Him through prayer. Prayer is the ultimate calling plan; you'll never get disconnected from Jesus if you pray and talk to Him. He will always be your best friend.

[Fade music.]

LESSON 35

Sick Survivor

Luke 5:17-26   Jesus Heals a Lame Man

Focus: God wants us to live healthy lives, full of His blessings, so that we may be a blessing and witness to others. Jesus came to break the power of sin and sickness in this world. Jesus is the One who heals us and makes us whole.

Characters:

    Jeff: a reality show host.
    Dominic DeKathlon: a healthy contestant.
    Ima B. Leever: the only Christian contestant.
    Two or three patients

Props: Handkerchief.

The Setup: Emergency room.

[Begin music.]

Announcer: *[Offstage]* This week on Sick Survivor, we're down to the final two. After 14 weeks of living and working in a hospital emergency room, 22 contestants have gone home. Only two healthy people are left: *[Dominic and Ima enter.]* Dominic DeKathlon and Ima B. Leever. Will this be the week that one of them finally falls victim to the many diseases and viruses here on *Sick Survivor*? Let's check in with our host, Jeff.

[Fade music. Jeff enters next to Dominic. Ima helps sick patients and prays for them as Jeff and Dominic talk.]

Jeff: Welcome to *Sick Survivor*, everyone. As you know, our two contestants haven't left this emergency room for 14 weeks. Despite a constant stream of runny noses, sneezes and flu patients, Dominic and Ima are still here and still healthy. How have you avoided getting sick, Dominic?

Dominic: It's all in the head, Jeff.

Jeff: Really?

Dominic: Really! The mind is very powerful. After years of practice, I've been able to force my mind to think healthy thoughts only.

Jeff: It seems to be working.

Dominic: I'm as healthy as a horse. *[Prepares to sneeze]* Ah, ah… Ah-CHOO!

Jeff: That's not a good sign, Dominic. You OK?

Dominic: *[Wipes nose with hanky]* I'm fine. It was just a little dust in the air that made me sneeze. *[Sneezes again]* Ah-CHOO!

Ima: *[Praying for a patient, quietly in the background]* Thank You for healing. In Jesus' name, amen. *[Patient gets up and joyfully exits.]*

Jeff: Do you have any other tips to staying

healthy around so many sick people?

Dominic: Yeah, stay away from them.

Jeff: Stay away from sick people in a hospital? Are you joking?

Dominic: No siree, Bob! I've stayed as far away from the patients as possible. Except for the challenges, I've had zero contact with the people here.

Jeff: Our challenges have definitely kept you busy. Which challenge was the hardest?

Dominic: Biohazard trash day was interesting, but the bedpan-changing relay was definitely the toughest. Ah, ah… *[Starts to sneeze, but stifles it]*

Jeff: Are you sure you're OK, Dominic?

Dominic: Perfectly fine. *[Big sneeze]* Ah-CHOO!

Jeff: I think you'd better have the doctors check you out while we talk with your competition. *[Dominic exits, and Jeff goes over to Ima, who just finished helping a patient.]* Ima, can we talk with you?

Ima: Sure, Jeff. I just finished praying with Mr. Jenkins.

Jeff: Fourteen weeks without a sniffle, Ima. How do you feel?

Ima: I feel great, and I'm blessed to be here. I've met so many wonderful people.

Jeff: You're always in a good mood, Ima. Is that what's kept you well?

Ima: Attitude is important, Jeff, but that's not why I'm still here.

Jeff: I noticed you were praying with that patient just now; is prayer your secret?

[Mr. Jenkins enters.]

Ima: That's part of it, Jeff. I talk to Jesus every day. After all, He's the Great Healer.

Jeff: Does that explain all the sick patients who left the hospital early? The doctors have noticed the effect your daily prayers have had on others.

Ima: The Bible says that the prayer offered in faith will make the sick person well (That's in James 5:15). I believe in Jesus, because He's the only One who can heal your inside and your outside.

Jeff: I don't get it.

Ima: Jesus forgave my sins and healed me from all the bad things in life. If He can take care of my inside, He can definitely take care of my outside, my body. Jesus came to earth to break the power of sin and sickness forever.

Jeff: So Jesus is the reason you're our winner, Ima?

Ima: Jesus is the reason for all good things, Jeff. But I didn't know I was the winner. I thought Dominic was still here.

Dominic: *[Enters coughing]* I am still here! And I'm fit as a fiddle! *[Sneezes]* Ah-CHOO!

Jeff: Sorry, Dominic. Our doctors say you're officially sick. That makes Ima the winner.

Dominic: It can't be. She must have cheated!

Ima: Dominic, the power of Jesus is the only thing that's healed me and made me whole. You could experience the same power, if you just give your life to Jesus. Let me pray with you!

Dominic: Aaagh! Get away from me! *[Sneezes]* Ah-choo! *[Exits quickly]*

Jeff: Looks like Ima found the way to win real immunity from sin and sickness. Back to you, Don.

[Jeff and Ima exit. Begin music.]

Announcer: Thanks, Jeff, and thank you, Ima. Well, folks, it's clear to see that Jesus helps us thrive, not just survive. Let Jesus heal you today—inside and out!

[Fade music.]

LESSON 36

The Doodad Gang and the Case of the Cut Off Connection

Luke 15:11–32   The Story of the Prodigal

Focus: As Christians, we need each other. We're a family, and families need to stay together in order to stay close. If we disconnect ourselves from God's family, we make an easy target for the enemy. God's people should always say, "I will stay connected to the family of God."

Characters:

Detective Doodad: a brilliant yet eccentric detective who somehow always has the right answer.
Henry: a younger boy who looks tough, but is gentle. Give him a computer, and he'll find your answer in no time.
Keona: a sensible and intelligent girl who likes to work things out.
Dr. D. Seaver: Detective Doodad's childhood friend and present-day archenemy, a master of disguise.

Props: Small plant.

The Setup: Small wooded area in the neighborhood.

[Begin music.]

Announcer: *[Offstage]* It's time again for the continuing adventures of Detective Doodad and the Doodad Gang! Detective Doodad and the gang are going on the offensive to try and locate Dr. D. Seaver's hideout. Teams of two have fanned out across the city to hunt down their elusive enemy.

[Detective Doodad, Henry and Keona enter. Fade music.]

Detective Doodad: Here we are. Just the place we're looking for.

Henry: Detective Doodad, it's a bunch of woods and bushes. Why do you think Dr. D. Seaver would be in here?

Detective Doodad: There are small, wooded areas like this all over the city, Henry. I think Dr. D. Seaver is using them to hide his movements.

Keona: So Dr. D. Seaver's hideout is probably in one of these areas.

Detective Doodad: Or the entrance to it is. Keep your eyes open for anything. It won't be easy finding clues here.

Henry: But it will be easy finding mosquitoes! *[Slaps his arm]*

Detective Doodad: This is a dangerous task, you two. It's very important that you stay connected with us at all times. Leave your communicators on; we don't want to get separated for any reason.

Keona: Where will you be, Detective?

Detective Doodad: I'll be on the next street over. Tony and Mindi Lee aren't far from here either, so call if you need us. Remember: Stay connected! *[Exits]*

Keona: You heard him, Henry. Let's stay together.

Henry: OK, but I want to check out these

bushes down here first. *[Henry exits. A plant shakes as though he's moving it.]*

Keona: Henry! We're supposed to stay together.

Henry: *[Offstage]* We are together. You're up there; I'm down here. Hey, I think I found a socket wrench!

Keona: I'm going to check out these trees to the left. Call me when you're done. *[Exits]*

Henry: *[Offstage]* OK! This is cool. There's all kinds of stuff down here. *[Re-enters]*

I'm gonna have to show Tony later. *[Speaks into wrist, but communicator is gone]* Keona, come in…Hey! Where's my communicator? It must have come off when I was searching. It must be here somewhere. *[Exits, and plant shakes.]*

Keona: *[Re-enters]* Nothing over there. Henry? Are you done yet? We have to keep moving.

Henry: *[Re-enters]* You go on, I'll be right there.

Keona: We're supposed to stick together, Henry.

Henry: Yeah, but I lost my communicator. I need to find it.

Keona: Do you want some help?

Henry: No, it's not a big deal.

Keona: It will be if the Detective finds out. I just called him. He wants us to meet them at the end of the street.

Henry: I know it's here somewhere.

Keona: Maybe we should call the others.

Henry: Keona, I'm OK. You go meet them, and tell them I'm on my way.

Keona: *[Unsure]* Don't be long… *[Exits]*

Henry: I can't believe this. *[Exits beside the bush]* Maybe it rolled down the hill.

Dr. D. Seaver: *[Appearing from behind the bush]* Well, well, well, what do we have here? *[He looks down.]* Shhhh! I think I've caught a little mouse at my front doorstep. Be careful little mouse, you might find that the big, bad cat is still at home! *[Looks around]* Someone's coming! I'd better hide. *[Exits]*

Detective Doodad: *[Enters]* Henry? Henry! Where are you?

Henry: *[Entering]* I'm here, Detective.

Detective Doodad: Keona told me about the lost communicator. Are you all right?

Henry: I'm fine, Detective Doodad, but I can't find it. I can't find my wrist communicator. I'm sorry.

Detective Doodad: We can get you another communicator, Henry. I'm more concerned about you not staying with Keona and the rest of us.

Henry: But there was all this cool stuff!

Detective Doodad: Henry, you have to

stay connected. Let us help you. It's too easy to get lost or hurt when you're all alone.

Henry: Yeah, you're right.

Detective Doodad: Come on, the others are waiting. Let's do this together, OK?

Henry: Yes, sir!

[Detective Doodad and Henry exit as Dr. D. Seaver enters with the wrist communicator.]

Dr. D. Seaver: Look what I found. It's Henry's little communicator. Finders keepers, losers weepers! This could prove very useful to me. I think I'm going to get connected…to the Doodad Gang! Ha, ha, ha!

[Exits. Begin music.]

Announcer: *[Offstage]* Henry learned an important lesson about staying connected. But will he remember it in the future? What evil plan does Dr. D. Seaver have in store for Detective Doodad? Stay tuned and see!

[Fade music.]

LESSON 37

Dr. D. Seaver Dupes the Doodad Gang

John 13:1-5, 12-17   Jesus Washes the Disciples' Feet

Focus: Jesus showed us how to live by showing us how to serve. God wants us to be an example; He loves it when we help others.

Characters:

Detective Doodad: a brilliant yet eccentric detective who somehow always has the right answer.
Tony: a natural leader who tends to jump in with both feet.
Henry: a younger boy who looks tough, but is gentle. Give him a computer, and he'll find your answer in no time.
Mindi Lee: the new girl in town. She's seemingly shy, but not afraid to fight for what's right.
Dr. D. Seaver: Detective Doodad's childhood friend and present-day archenemy, a master of disguise.

Props: Paper grocery sack, apple, wig and shawl.

The Setup: A wooded area in the neighborhood. Dr. D. Seaver appears in this skit disguised as an elderly woman in a wig and shawl.

[Begin music.]

Announcer: *[Offstage]* Welcome back to the adventures of Detective Doodad and the Doodad Gang! Good news: Detective Doodad and his helpers are hot on the trail of the evil Dr. D. Seaver. The bad news is: Dr. D. Seaver found Henry's lost communicator, so he knows what they're doing. They'll need all the help they can get when he tries to spring his trap on the unsuspecting Doodad Gang.

[Detective Doodad, Tony, Henry and Mindi Lee enter. Fade music.]

Detective Doodad: All right everyone, I know we're on the hunt for Dr. D. Seaver, but let's not forget why we're here. We're here to help people.

Henry: We'll help a lot of people by capturing Dr. D. Seaver.

Tony: We've been searching these woods for days and haven't seen any sign of him.

Henry: Yeah, it's like he left town.

Mindi Lee: Or he knows we're looking for him.

Detective Doodad: That's good thinking, Mindi Lee. But Dr. D. Seaver knows we won't give up. I'm going to meet Keona at the end of the street. You three start searching, and remember: being a helper pleases God. *[Exits]*

Tony: OK gang, let's split up. We'll cover more ground that way.

Mindi Lee: Leave your communicators on, and check in every minute.

Henry: *[Looking at his wrist]* Oh no, not again!

Tony: What's the matter, Henry?

Henry: You know that new communicator

Detective Doodad gave me?

Mindi Lee: Please tell us you didn't forget to put it on this morning.

Henry: OK...I didn't forget to put it on this morning!

Tony: Oh man, this is too funny!

Mindi Lee: It's not something to laugh at, Tony.

Henry: I'm in big trouble.

Tony: No, you're not. The Detective wants us to help others, right?

Henry: Yeah, so?

Tony: So I'm going to help you out. You and Mindi Lee start looking while I run back and get your new communicator.

Henry: You'd do that for me? You're the best friend in the whole world, Tony!

Mindi Lee: Be sure to let Keona know where you are, Tony.

Tony: No problem. Don't catch Dr. D. Seaver without me! *[Exits]*

Henry: What are we looking for, Mindi Lee?

Mindi Lee: The Detective believes Dr. D. Seaver has an underground hideout. He thinks there are tunnels that will lead us there.

Henry: So we're looking for the entrance, right?

Mindi Lee: That's right. Keep your eyes on the ground.

Henry: OK.

[Dr. D. Seaver, disguised as an elderly woman, enters, carrying a paper grocery sack.]

Dr. D. Seaver: *[Disguised voice]* Oh, I wish there was someone to help me with my groceries.

Henry: *[Sees the woman]* We can help you, ma'am. Come on, Mindi Lee.

Dr. D. Seaver: That's very helpful of you young people. *[Henry takes the sack.]* Why don't you try a bite of this lovely apple, my dear?

Mindi Lee: Yes, ma'am. *[Mindi Lee takes a bite of the apple as Henry looks on.]*

Dr. D. Seaver: It's good, isn't it?

Mindi Lee: I guess so. *[Faintly]* I don't feel so well. Henry...call...Detective... *[Faints]*

[Mindi Lee falls out of sight as Dr. D. Seaver reveals himself.]

Dr. D. Seaver: Hello, Henry. I guess an apple a day doesn't keep the Doctor away, now does it?

Henry: Dr. D. Seaver! You drugged her!

Dr. D. Seaver: Of course I did. I couldn't let her find my hideout now, could I?

Henry: What do you want?

Dr. D. Seaver: Just you, my boy. You're coming with me!

[Dr. D. Seaver exits, pushing Henry. Tony enters on the other side.]

Tony: Henry? Mindi Lee? That's odd. I told Keona they'd be right here.

Mindi Lee: *[Offstage, weakly]* Tony…help!

Tony: Whoa! Mindi Lee! Are you OK?

[Detective Doodad enters.]

Detective Doodad: What's going on here?

Mindi Lee: It was Dr. D. Seaver. He…he took Henry!

Tony: I knew I shouldn't have left you two. I was only trying to help!

Detective Doodad: We'll sort this out later. Right now, we've got to help Henry. And the first thing we need to do is pray!

[Everyone exits. Begin music.]

Announcer: *[Offstage]* As Detective Doodad led in prayer, Henry was taken to the evil Doctor's hideout. Henry and Tony were good helpers; unfortunately, Henry walked right into Dr. D. Seaver's trap. Can Henry escape? Can the Doodad Gang help free their friend? Tune in next time to find out!

[Fade music.]

Power Stan Finds His Voice

Acts 2:1–18 The Early Christians Preach the Gospel

Focus: You don't have to be a superhero to share the good news of Jesus. Trust in God and His Spirit to give you the words to say in your own way. God gives you the power to share Jesus with others.

Characters:

Stanley: a boy who's timid about sharing the gospel.
Marcus: Stanley's Christian friend.

Props: Red superhero mask, red cape, and cardboard with "PS" written on the front and masking tape on back.

The Setup: Anywhere.

[Begin music.]

Announcer: *[Offstage]* Welcome, everyone. Today you're going to meet Stanley. Stanley knows Jesus, and he wants to tell others about God, but he has a problem: Stanley's shy. Stanley thinks he has to know all the right things to say before he can say the right thing. Let's see if Stanley can find his voice for Jesus.

[Fade music. Stanley enters, pacing back and forth.]

Stanley: Hmmm, I could create a Web page online for people to look at. *[Pause]* No, I'd still have to talk. *[Pause]* I know. I could rent an airplane and write "Jesus loves you" in the clouds.

[Marcus enters.]

Marcus: Hey, Stanley.

Stanley: Oh, hi, Marcus!

Marcus: Who are you talking to?

Stanley: Nobody. I was just talking out loud.

Marcus: I do that sometimes.

Stanley: Yeah, I'm trying to come up with some good ideas, and if I say them out loud, one of them might sound good.

Marcus: What kind of ideas are you looking for?

Stanley: I'd rather not say.

Marcus: Stanley, I'm your friend. Let me help you.

Stanley: You promise you won't laugh?

Marcus: I promise, no laughing. What's the problem?

Stanley: My problem is that I don't know how to tell people about God.

Marcus: It's not hard. You just talk to people.

Stanley: See, that's the problem. You don't have a problem talking to people. But I get tongue-tied when they ask me what time it is.

Marcus: But you talk to me OK.

Stanley: That's because I know you. I'm shy in front of people I don't know. Remember Stephanie's birthday party?

Marcus: Oh, yeah. You wouldn't even sing "Happy Birthday."

Stanley: Wouldn't sing? I couldn't sing. I was so nervous, I forgot the words.

Marcus: Have you come up with any ideas for how you can tell people about God?

Stanley: Lots! But I don't know if any of them are good.

Marcus: Let me hear one.

Stanley: OK, here's one: I get a big car and write the entire Book of John on the hood. Then people can stop and read it at the traffic light.

Marcus: Only one problem.

Stanley: What's that?

Marcus: You're not old enough to drive.

Stanley: Oh yeah, I forgot. OK, here's my best idea so far. *[Turns and exits]*

Marcus: Walking away? That's not a good idea.

Stanley: *[Offstage]* I'm not walking away; I had to put it on to show it to you. Are you ready?

Marcus: I'm ready.

Stanley: OK. Hit it, Mr. Announcer!

[Stan enters wearing a red cape and mask, with "PS" on his chest.]

Announcer: *[Offstage]* Look, up in the sky; it's a bird, it's a plane, it's Power Stan! All-powerful witness from a spiritual dimension, Power Stan is here!

Marcus: You're a superhero?

Stanley: *[Louder voice]* Yes! When I wear this, I'm "Power Stan," all-powerful witness for God.

Marcus: Do you have any special powers?

Stanley: *[Still loud]* Yes! I can memorize books of the Bible at one glance. I can speak loudly in a big voice, and best of all, I can tell people about Jesus faster than a speeding bullet! *[Normal voice]* What do you think?

Marcus: Well, the costume would attract a lot of attention, but you don't need it.

Stanley: I don't?

Marcus: Nah. You don't need to be a superhero to tell people about Jesus. And you don't need to have a big voice or a flashy costume. Just tell them what Jesus has done for you.

Stanley: But what if I don't know the people?

Marcus: Then take time to become their friend before you introduce them to your friend Jesus.

Stanley: I never thought of that before.

Marcus: And don't worry about what to say. God's Spirit will give you His words and His power. Just ask Him.

Stanley: I don't need a costume to find a voice for God! God can use my voice.

Marcus: That's right!

Stanley: Power Stan is done, but Jesus, the real "Power Man," is number one!

[Stanley and Marcus exit. Begin music.]

Announcer: *[Offstage]* Even though "Power Stan" is gone for good, in his place is someone much more powerful: Stanley, the boy believer with a voice for Jesus. Stanley found out that God can use us just as we are, if we let Him. God will give us all the power we need.

[Fade music.]

LESSON 40

Detective Doodad and the Missing Member

Acts 3:1–20   The Miracle at the Gate

Focus: As children of God, we have inherited His power. Jesus' triumph over sin has given us the right to act in His name. God gives us authority in the name of Jesus.

Characters:

Detective Doodad: a brilliant yet eccentric detective who somehow always has the right answer.
Tony: a natural leader who tends to jump in with both feet.
Keona: a sensible and intelligent girl who likes to work things out.
Mindi Lee: the new girl in town. She's seemingly shy, but not afraid to fight for what's right.
Officer Fogg: a headstrong policeman who doesn't listen.

Props: Flashlights (optional).

The Setup: The Doodad Gang heads up a search party in the area Henry was found missing.

[Begin music.]

Announcer: *[Offstage]* Time now for the continuing adventures of Detective Doodad and the Doodad Gang! Henry is still missing, after being kidnapped by the evil Dr. D. Seaver. Detective Doodad and the others have been praying and searching for Henry all day, and now they're waiting for the police teams to help search for their missing team member.

[Fade music. Detective Doodad, Tony, Keona and Mindi Lee enter.]

Tony: I can't believe Henry was kidnapped. Dr. D. Seaver has him locked away somewhere.

Mindi Lee: How do you think I feel, Tony? I was there when Dr. D. Seaver showed up in disguise. We thought he was a grandmother. I should have known better.

Detective Doodad: Neither of you have any reason to feel guilty. Dr. D. Seaver planned the whole thing.

Keona: Detective Doodad is right. Dr. D. Seaver was going to kidnap someone, and he did.

Tony: So how do we rescue Henry?

Detective Doodad: With faith and prayer, and some help from our friends.

Keona: I think the police are here, Detective!

[Officer Fogg enters.]

Officer: Good evening, Detective, SIR! I'm Officer Fogg.

Detective Doodad: Hello, officer. Thanks for coming.

Officer: Our pleasure, SIR! We've got six squads ready to go. What would you like us to do?

Detective Doodad: I want the teams to split up and start searching the wooded areas first. I think Dr. D. Seaver has been using underground tunnels to move around the city. I'll lead the teams myself.

Officer: Very good, SIR!

Detective Doodad: You don't have to shout, officer.

Officer: Right you are, SIR! Which team would you like me to lead?

Detective Doodad: Officer Fogg, as I said, I'll lead the search teams. I want you to assist the Doodad Gang in searching the spot where Henry was taken.

Officer: So you want me to lead the Doodad Gang? Yes, SIR!

Detective Doodad: No officer, listen to me. Tony, Keona and Mindi Lee know that area very well. In fact, Mindi Lee was there when Henry was taken. I want you to assist them. I'm putting Mindi Lee in charge, is that clear?

Officer: Yes, SIR!

Mindi Lee: You're putting me in charge, Detective Doodad?

Detective Doodad: Mindi Lee, you were there when Henry was taken, and no one knows that area better than you do. You have my authority to lead this team.

Mindi Lee: If you say so.

Detective Doodad: Don't be afraid to give orders. You're in charge.

Officer: Let's get going, kids! There's no time to waste.

[*Everyone exits.*]

Announcer: [*Offstage*] And so Mindi Lee, Tony and Keona set off with Officer Fogg to search the woods. Mindi Lee is in charge, but does she know it? See if you think her actions show it.

[*Officer Fogg, Mindi Lee, Tony and Keona enter.*]

Officer: OK, let's start here.

Tony: This doesn't look like the spot.

Keona: That's because it isn't. Dr. D. Seaver grabbed Henry on the other side of that hill.

Mindi Lee: Officer, we need to start over there.

Officer: [*Condescending*] It's all right, Mindi Lee, we'll get there soon enough. You just sit back and let me handle this. [*Exits*]

Tony: That guy doesn't get it. We're in the wrong place.

Keona: You need to do something, Mindi Lee. The Detective put you in charge.

Mindi Lee: What can I do, Keona?

Tony: Be a leader. Use the power you have to get the job done.

Officer: *[Re-enters]* I found a few clues I want to check out here, kids.

Mindi Lee: Officer Fogg, we're going to where Henry was taken. Right now.

Officer: No, Mindi Lee, we need to look around here first.

Mindi Lee: I wasn't asking, officer. Let's go.

Officer: I'm in charge here, miss.

Mindi Lee: *[Sternly]* No, you're not, Officer Fogg. You may be older than me, but Detective Doodad gave me the authority to lead this team. I know what we're looking for. We're going, and that's an order. Do you understand?

Officer: *[Taken aback]* Uh…yes, MA'AM! *[He exits.]*

Tony: Way to go, Mindi Lee!

Mindi Lee: Thanks. Let's go, guys.

Tony and Keona: Yes, MA'AM!

[Everyone exits. Begin music.]

Announcer: *[Offstage]* Mindi Lee learned an important lesson about using the authority given to her. We've also been given power by God to share Jesus with others. All we have to do is to not be afraid to use it. Tune in next time for the continuing adventures of the Doodad Gang!

[Fade music.]

LESSON 41

The Doodad Gang and the Place of Persecution

Acts 6:8-15; 7:54-60   Stephen's Persecution

Focus: Jesus came to change the world. Some people don't like to change, and those are the kind of people who hated Jesus. They hated the followers of Jesus as much as they hated Him. Like the early Christians, if you live for Jesus, you will face persecution.

Characters:

Detective Doodad: a brilliant yet eccentric detective who somehow always has the right answer.
Tony: a natural leader who tends to jump in with both feet.
Keona: a sensible and intelligent girl who likes to work things out.
Henry: a younger boy who looks tough, but is gentle. Give him a computer, and he'll find your answer in no time.
Mindi Lee: the new girl in town. She's seemingly shy, but not afraid to fight for what's right.
Dr. D. Seaver: Detective Doodad's childhood friend and present-day archenemy, a master of disguise.

Props: Rope.

The Setup: The woods; Dr. D. Seaver's hideout.

[Begin music.]

Announcer: *[Offstage]* Welcome again to the adventures of Detective Doodad and the Doodad Gang! Despite their best efforts, Detective Doodad and the Doodad Gang haven't been able to locate their friend Henry. The Detective and the gang have camped out where Henry was kidnapped. Henry's friends refuse to give up the search.

[Fade music. Detective Doodad, Tony, Keona and Mindi Lee enter.]

Mindi Lee: It's raining.

Tony: Again?

Keona: We won't find many new clues in this downpour. The rain just washes everything away.

Tony: I wish the last few days could be washed away.

Detective Doodad: The rain will stop, Tony. Sometimes it's hard to do the right thing. God never said there wouldn't be problems. But I thank the Lord that Henry has good friends like you.

Keona: We'll find him, Detective Doodad. I know it.

Tony: Yeah, we're not going to leave or stop praying for Henry.

Mindi Lee: We'll stick together, Detective. He'd do the same for us.

Detective Doodad: I know, Mindi Lee. This area must be the key. I think that's why Henry was taken. He must have gotten close to finding Dr. D. Seaver's hideout.

Tony: These woods are close to everything in town.

Mindi Lee: Maybe we haven't seen Dr. D. Seaver because he can't come out.

Keona: Yeah! Maybe he's trapped or afraid of

being seen.

Detective Doodad: That's good thinking. But what could be keeping Dr. D. Seaver trapped?

[Detective Doodad, Tony, Keona and Mindi Lee exit.]

Announcer: *[Offstage]* Meanwhile, beneath the city, Dr. D. Seaver is trying to get Henry to talk. His patience is wearing thin—with Henry, and especially with the weather.

[Dr. D. Seaver enters, leading Henry by a rope.]

Dr. D. Seaver: Rain, rain, go away, and don't come back another day! I can't believe this rain. The soggy soil has collapsed all of my tunnels, except for one.

Henry: I hope all your tunnels cave in.

Dr. D. Seaver: Be careful what you wish for, boy. That tunnel is our only way out.

Henry: Then why don't you just leave, Dr. D. Seaver?

Dr. D. Seaver: I'd love to, but guess who's pitched his tent near the entryway?

Henry: Detective Doodad!

Dr. D. Seaver: Yes, the Defective Detective has turned my doorstep into a campground. The next thing you know, they'll be toasting marshmallows.

Henry: They'll get you soon!

Dr. D. Seaver: *[In Henry's face]* Henry, there's only one reason I've kept you around: I want to know about the Detective's inventions. Are you going to tell me?

Henry: For the last time, no! I won't tell you anything.

Dr. D. Seaver: You're such a goody-goody two-shoes, Henry. You should leave that stupid gang. It's dumb.

Henry: Detective Doodad isn't dumb. He's my friend. And so are all the others.

Dr. D. Seaver: Some friends. I'm sure they've promised to rescue you, but that hasn't happened, has it? On the other hand, I always keep my promises.

Henry: Yeah, right.

Dr. D. Seaver: It's true. In fact, I promise you that if you tell me about those wonderful toys of the Detective, I'll let you go.

Henry: You'll let me go?

Dr. D. Seaver: Yes, and I'll never bother you again. Just tell me what I want to know.

Henry: I can't.

Dr. D. Seaver: Of course you can. If you don't, I'll be forced to kidnap another one of your friends.

Henry: *[Angrily]* You're an evil man, Dr. D. Seaver!

Dr. D. Seaver: Flattery will get you nowhere, boy. Do what I say, or else!

Henry: I'll never turn on Detective Doodad—never!

[Sounds of water dripping]

Dr. D. Seaver: I'm going to let you think about that, Henry. But don't take too long; the roof is starting to sag under the weight of all that rain. Obey me, and I'll get you out. Otherwise, I'll have to leave you here. It's your choice! *[Exits]*

Henry: I need help. *[Praying]* Lord, I know that hard times come, and I know I'm here because I've stood up against evil. But I need your help, Lord. Help my friends and give them strength. Help me to stay strong for you. Amen. *[Exits as music begins]*

Announcer: *[Offstage]* Henry is being persecuted for standing up to evil. But for Henry, living for Jesus is not an option; he knows the right thing to do. But will he turn on his friends—just this once—to save himself? Will he tell Dr. D. Seaver what he knows? Can Detective Doodad and the Doodad Gang find their friend in time? Tune in next time!

[Fade music.]

The Spirit's Most Wanted

Galatians 5:22-23   The Fruit of the Spirit

Focus: Because we are connected to Jesus, His Spirit lives in us and helps us to develop strong character traits that make us look more like Him. We know these as the fruits of the Spirit.

Characters:

   Narrator: a female who directs the others as they enter and exit.

   Five boys and five girls: each represents a fruit of the Spirit.

Note: If you don't have nine hand puppets, this is an excellent script to use "mops" puppetry. In this type of rod puppetry, a mop or broom becomes the "head" of the puppet. You can create a face and eyes by hot-gluing felt or fun foam shapes to the head. Let the kids create their own faces for the puppets. Attach the signs to the "body" (wooden handle) of the puppets. The puppeteers walk the characters in and out.

Props: Nine shirts or signs, one for each puppet: LOVE, JOY, PEACE, PATIENCE, KINDNESS, GOODNESS, FAITHFULNESS, GENTLENESS, and SELF-CONTROL.

The Setup: Anywhere. Consider keeping a beat in the background as puppets say their lines.

[Begin music. Narrator enters.]

Narrator: Hello, boys and girls. Today we're going to meet nine characters who are "Wanted"—in fact, they're on God's "Most Wanted" list. These characters show up when God's Spirit lives in us. I'll have them enter, one by one, and they'll tell you a little about themselves. Let's start with LOVE. *[Narrator exits.]*

[Fade music.]

LOVE: *[Enters]*
Hello, everyone, my name is LOVE
I come straight from the Lord above
You all know me, yes, you do
God is love; He put me in you!
When Jesus lives in your heart to stay
Love fills your life every day
You'll love others, as you should
And tell your friends God's love is good.
[Exits]

JOY: *[Enters]*
My name is JOY for a happy soul
Jesus came to make you whole
You will sing and shout "Hurray!"
Living for God is the only way!
So jump right up, shout His praise
Joy can fill up all your days
You'll feel so good you can't sit down
God's joy makes smiles from every frown.
[Exits]

PEACE: *[Enters]*
They call me PEACE, and it's nice to hear
The peace of God drives out all fear
Peace can calm each heart and mind
A quiet place everyone can find
A peaceful valley, a hidden stream
The peace of God is like a dream
Even in the crazy times
The Spirit of Peace protects your mind.
[Exits]

PATIENCE: *[Enters]*
I'm PATIENCE, I'll teach you to wait
On God's time, His plan is great
Patience helps you, yes it's true
The Spirit of God will give it to you.
Learning to wait for God to say when
What to do, and who to send
He will guide you for His glory
Patience is one more part of the story. *[Exits]*

KINDNESS: *[Enters]*
KINDNESS I am, and kind you'll be
When you treat people respectfully
Love your neighbor as yourself
Put others first, it's always a help!
Giving a gift or writing a note
Helping someone to build a boat
Taking the time to be a friend
Kindness is giving that never ends *[Exits]*

GOODNESS: *[Enters]*
They call me GOODNESS, choose me too
Good or bad, it's up to you
If Jesus lives inside your heart
He will help you make the choice that's smart.
The Spirit leads and you can follow
Other ways will leave you hollow
God is good so don't delay
Say no to evil every day. *[Exits]*

FAITHFULNESS: *[Enters]*
I'm FAITHFULNESS, trusting God for real
You walk by faith and that's the deal
Faith in God will grow and grow
Trust in Him and your faith will show
Lean on Him and not your own ways
He will lead you all your days
Faith pleases God you will see
By faith you'll live eternally. *[Exits]*

GENTLENESS: *[Enters]*
I'm GENTLENESS, not loud or pushy
A still, small voice, but not real mushy
God can speak in gentle tones
He doesn't need to rattle your bones.
The Spirit will teach you gentleness
To help your friends who feel some stress
Take it from a gentle person
Gentleness calms, and that's for certain. *[Exits]*

SELF-CONTROL: *[Enters]*
About SELF-CONTROL I'm the expert
Control yourself it doesn't hurt
A life of blessings you will find
When God controls your body and mind
If you want to break the grip of sin
God can teach you discipline
The Spirit helps, when control you seek
He gives you strength when you are weak. *[Exits]*

[Narrator re-enters. Begin music.]

Narrator: Love, joy, peace and patience, kindness, goodness, faithfulness, gentleness, and don't forget self-control. These are what you'll start to see when God's own Spirit works in your life. Your character will start to change as the Spirit rearranges. Let God put what is "most wanted" into your life!

[Narrator exits. Fade music.]

LESSON 47

Detective Doodad Sticks to It and Gets His Man

Philippians 4:10-20   The Unlimited Potential in Every Christian

Focus: The world is full of obstacles for those who believe in God. Jesus will give you the power to overcome the world. Through Christ, you can do all things.

Characters:

Detective Doodad: a brilliant yet eccentric detective who somehow always has the right answer.
Tony: a natural leader who tends to jump in with both feet.
Keona: a sensible and intelligent girl who likes to work things out.
Henry: a younger boy who looks tough, but is gentle. Give him a computer, and he'll find your answer in no time.
Mindi Lee: the new girl in town. She's seemingly shy, but not afraid to fight for what's right.
Dr. D. Seaver: Detective Doodad's childhood friend and present-day archenemy, a master of disguise.

Props: Prop table with wrist communicator on it.

The Setup: Detective Doodad's camp and Dr. D. Seaver's hideout.

[Begin music.]

Announcer: *[Offstage]* Time now for the continuing adventures of Detective Doodad and the Doodad Gang! A determined Doodad Gang continues to search for the kidnapped Henry. Dr. D. Seaver, however, still holds Henry captive deep in his underground hideout.

[Fade music. Detective Doodad, Tony, Keona and Mindi Lee enter.]

Detective Doodad: We're getting close to finding Henry and Dr. D. Seaver.

Tony: I feel it, too, Detective. The tunnel to Dr. D. Seaver's hideout is around here somewhere.

Keona: Now that the rain has stopped, the search has gone much faster.

Detective Doodad: Are the police teams in place?

Mindi Lee: Yes, Detective Doodad. They're surrounding this entire area.

Detective Doodad: Good. Dr. D. Seaver is going to have to come out soon. And we'll be waiting for him.

Mindi Lee: I'll call the police and let them know we're in position.

Tony: How's the new invention coming, Detective Doodad?

Detective Doodad: I finished the "Sticky Shoes" last night, Tony. I can't wait to stomp on the evil things Dr. D. Seaver has done! Everyone, don't forget that we can do all things in Christ. I know Henry hasn't forgotten.

[Detective Doodad, Tony and Keona exit. Mindi Lee speaks into her communicator.]

Mindi Lee: Police command center, this is Mindi Lee of the Doodad Gang, over. *[Exits. Offstage]* All units are in position. Henry, if you can hear this, hold on. We're coming to get you.

[A tied-up Henry *appears next to a prop table. Henry's wrist communicator is lying on the table, and he hears* Mindi Lee's *message.]*

Henry: *[Struggling]* I hear you, Mindi Lee. If I could just reach…my…communicator. *[Relaxes]* I've loosened the straps, but I still can't get my hand free. I've got to get out of here.

Dr. D. Seaver: *[Entering]* That meddling Doodad Gang. They're camped out right next to my tunnel, and there are police everywhere!

Henry: Detective Doodad is going to find you, Dr. D. Seaver.

Dr. D. Seaver: I don't think so. He's not that smart, Henry. None of you are. But you keep hoping if you want; I have better things to do. *[Exits]*

Henry: Okay, now's my chance. Help me, Lord. I know I can do all things in Christ. Please give me the strength. *[Henry struggles.]* Almost free! Just a little more. *[Henry gets one arm free.]* There! Now I can call the gang! *[He reaches for the communicator.]* Detective Doodad! Can you hear me?

[Detective Doodad appears on the upper level.]

Detective Doodad: Henry! Is that you?

Henry: Yes, Detective. Dr. D. Seaver's got me tied up in his hideout. He says you're right next to his tunnel!

Detective Doodad: I knew it! Hang on, Henry. I'll be there soon. *[Exits]*

Dr. D. Seaver: *[Enters]* Bad news, Henry. The police are a little too close for comfort. You and I are going to take a little trip.

Henry: I'm not going anywhere with you.

Dr. D. Seaver: Don't be afraid, you'll be asleep the whole time. Especially after I give you this sleeping pill.

Henry: Stay away from me!

Dr. D. Seaver: It'll all be over in a second, Henry.

[Detective Doodad bursts in.]

Detective Doodad: It's all over now, Dr. D. Seaver! Get away from Henry right now!

Dr. D. Seaver: *[Surprised]* How did you find me?

Detective Doodad: I told you I'd stop you. Give it up, Doctor.

Dr. D. Seaver: I'm still too slippery for you to catch, Detective!

Detective Doodad: Not for long. Go, go, Doodad Sticky Shoes!

[Detective Doodad runs back and forth across the front of the stage. His shoes make squishy sounds.]

Henry: Detective Doodad, why are you running around Dr. D. Seaver?

Detective Doodad: Because I've trapped him. Don't try to cross my sticky shoe trail, Doctor.

Dr. D. Seaver: What? My feet! I can't move. I'm stuck! Aaaagh!

Detective Doodad: Detective Doodad to police command center. Dr. D. Seaver is in custody. You can move in now.

Henry: Detective Doodad, you did it! You captured Dr. D. Seaver.

Detective Doodad: We can do all things through Christ, Henry. Let's go find the others.

[Both exit. Begin music.]

Announcer: *[Offstage]* A cheer goes up in Techno City as Dr. D. Seaver is finally captured. Henry learned that in Christ, he has the power to do anything. Jesus overcame the world to give us the power to succeed. Three cheers for Jesus, who makes all things possible!

[Fade music.]

LESSON 50

Dr. D. Seaver Gets What He Asks For

James 3:1–10

The Power of the Tongue

Focus: Words are powerful. Out of the same mouth come blessings and curses, and that's not right. God wants us to be in control of our words, because they can get us into a lot of trouble. What we say determines our way.

Characters:

Detective Doodad: a brilliant yet eccentric detective who somehow always has the right answer.

Mindi Lee: the new girl in town. She's seemingly shy, but not afraid to fight for what's right.

Henry: a younger boy who looks tough, but is gentle. Give him a computer, and he'll find your answer in no time.

Dr. D. Seaver: Detective Doodad's childhood friend and present-day archenemy, a master of disguise.

The Setup: City Jail (Cardboard set of bars separating Dr. D. Seaver from Detective Doodad). Option: Put Dr. D. Seaver on the lower level, with the visitors above.

[Begin music.]

Announcer: *[Offstage]* Time now for another adventure with Detective Doodad and the Doodad Gang! All of Techno City is breathing easy, now that Dr. D. Seaver is safely behind bars. The evil Doctor is being held under the highest security possible, and only Detective Doodad and the Doodad Gang are allowed to visit.

[Fade music. Dr. D. Seaver enters behind the jail bars. Detective Doodad enters.]

Dr. D. Seaver: Well, well, well, if it isn't the great Detective Doodad. You've come to celebrate my capture, no doubt.

Detective Doodad: Spare me the self-pity, Dr. D. Seaver. You knew I'd never let you continue your evil ways.

Dr. D. Seaver: I should have left town, rather than let a "meatball" like you capture me.

Detective Doodad: That's very insulting, Doctor.

Dr. D. Seaver: Oh, go soak your socks in the river, Detective. I may be in jail, but I don't have to listen to you lecture me. I'll say what I want, when I want, so there!

Detective Doodad: It's your choice, Dr. D. Seaver, but if I were you, I'd think about all the other bad choices you've made.

Dr. D. Seaver: The only bad choice I made is letting you catch me.

Detective Doodad: I'm not here to argue with you, Doctor. I came to ask you a question.

Dr. D. Seaver: A question?

Detective Doodad: Dr. D. Seaver, there are two young people out in the hall who have asked to talk to you. I told them I'd let them. But I'm asking you to watch what you say. Can you do that?

Dr. D. Seaver: Maybe I will, and maybe I won't.

Detective Doodad: Come in, Henry and Mindi Lee.

[Henry and Mindi Lee enter.]

Dr. D. Seaver: Henry? Mindi Lee? I should have known.

Mindi Lee: We meet again, Dr. D. Seaver.

Dr. D. Seaver: Unfortunately, yes.

Henry: How are you?

Dr. D. Seaver: Awful. How do you think I am, you silly boy? The food stinks, the bed is lumpy, and there's no TV.

Detective Doodad: Watch your words, Dr. D. Seaver.

Dr. D. Seaver: What in the world do you two want?

Henry: I wanted to tell you that I forgive you.

Mindi Lee: Me too. I forgive you, Dr. D. Seaver.

Dr. D. Seaver: *[Laughs aloud]* Ha, ha, ha! You forgive me? That's the funniest thing I've heard since I got here! Forgive me for what?

Mindi Lee: I forgive you for knocking me out in the woods.

Henry: And I forgive you for kidnapping me.

Dr. D. Seaver: *[Falsely]* Well, isn't that sweet. I don't know whether to laugh or cry.

Detective Doodad: Hear them out, Dr. D. Seaver. You might just learn something.

Henry: Mindi Lee and I wanted to let you know that we don't hate you, even if you did try to hurt us.

Mindi Lee: Yes. We wanted to say we forgive you, and we're praying for you.

Detective Doodad: You see, Dr. D. Seaver, words can help, or they can hurt. Your words are mean and hateful, because your heart is full of evil. Mindi Lee and Henry have said good things to you. Wouldn't you like to start using your tongue for good words too, Dr. D. Seaver?

Dr. D. Seaver: *[Pause]* I suppose I could apologize. But I won't.

Detective Doodad: Until you realize you need to change, Dr. D. Seaver, your life will always be sad.

Dr. D. Seaver: Detective, I'd like to ask a favor.

Detective Doodad: Yes?

Dr. D. Seaver: I'd like to ask that you don't visit anymore.

Detective Doodad: It's your choice, Dr. D. Seaver. We won't visit if you don't want us to. But we will always pray for you.

Henry: Me too. I'll pray for you, Dr. D. Seaver.

Dr. D. Seaver: Fair enough. They're taking me back to my cell now. Good-bye. *[He exits.]*

Mindi Lee: He's a very sad man.

Detective Doodad: And a very angry one. That's why he says bad things. But I'm proud of you, Henry and Mindi Lee. God is happy when we speak good words to others.

Henry: Do you think Dr. D. Seaver will ever change, Detective?

Detective Doodad: I don't know, Henry, but I do know this. God never stops loving us, no matter what we do. Let's go find Tony and Keona and get some ice cream, OK?

Henry and Mindi Lee: OK!

[Everyone exits. Begin music.]

Announcer: *[Offstage]* And so, Detective Doodad closes the case on the evil Dr. D. Seaver, who could never quite tame his tongue. What new adventures await the gang in the future? Only time will tell all that God has planned in the continuing story of Detective Doodad and the Doodad Gang!

[Fade music.]

LESSON 51

He Gave Me the Gifts That I Give

1 Peter 4:7–11   Using Your God-Given Gifts

Focus: God has made each of us special, with special gifts to use for His glory. It's up to us to use all the talents God has given us to help build up others. We can also use our talents to worship God and share His love. The point is to use your gifts. Everyone has special gifts from God.

Characters:

Marissa: a little girl who wants to know where her abilities came from.
Mom: Marissa's mom.
Brian: Marissa's friend.
Ashley: another of Marissa's friends.

The Setup: Anywhere.

[Begin music.]

Announcer: *[Offstage]* What are your gifts? God has given everyone special talents. Today we're going to meet Marissa. Marissa is a special little girl who can do many wonderful things. Let's see what she thinks when she finds out where those gifts came from.

[Fade music. Marissa enters, singing "Hey! Jesus Loves Me" from The Next Generation Praise *CD.]*

Marissa: *[Singing]* "Hey! Jesus loves me… Hey! Jesus loves me… Hey! Jesus loves me! The greatest thing that there could ever be is that Jesus loves me. Na na, na na, na na na na na. Na na, na na… I love to sing. But how did I learn to sing? I've never gone to singing lessons. Hmmm.

[Brian enters.]

Brian: Hi, Marissa. What are you doing?

Marissa: Hi Brian. I was singing, but now I'm thinking.

Brian: Thinking? What are you thinking about?

Marissa: About how I learned to sing.

Brian: Did your mom teach you?

Marissa: No. Mom says I started singing as soon as I could talk.

Brian: Maybe your dad taught you.

Marissa: Dad can't sing. Mom says I've been teaching him.

Brian: Oh. I don't know then. Maybe you could ask your mom who taught you how to sing.

Marissa: I think I will. Thanks, Brian. Bye! *[Exits]*

[Brian exits the other way. Ashley enters, then Marissa.]

Ashley: Hi, Marissa.

Marissa: Hi, Ashley. Hey, do you know who taught me how to sing?

Ashley: I didn't know you took lessons.

Marissa: I don't take lessons. I just know how to sing.

Ashley: Well I can sing, too, and nobody taught me.

Marissa: Yeah, how does that work?

Ashley: My mom says I have the voice of an angel. Maybe an angel gave me her voice so I could use it.

Marissa: Maybe. I don't know. This is a hard question. I'm going to ask my mom. *[Exits]*

Ashley: Yeah. Moms know everything. *[Exits]*

[Marissa's Mom enters, then Marissa.]

Mom: Hi, sweetheart.

Marissa: Mom, I have a big question. It's been in my brain all day, and now my head hurts because it wants to get out.

Mom: Well then you'd better let it out, honey. What's your question?

Marissa: Who taught me how to sing?

Mom: No one, sweetie. You just know how to sing.

Marissa: But how? Ashley says an angel gave her the voice she has.

Mom: It wasn't an angel who gave you the ability to sing. It was God.

Marissa: I didn't know God gave singing lessons.

Mom: Oh yes, God gives singing lessons and a whole lot more. God gives everyone special gifts of their own.

Marissa: Special gifts? You mean like Christmas gifts?

Mom: Much better than that, Marissa. God gives different talents to different people so that we can put them all together to praise Him.

Marissa: What kind of talents?

Mom: Well, your singing is a gift. There are lots of gifts. Some people can teach; some are great at sports; some are very smart; some people have the gift of encouraging others, and some are great at organizing things. All of these are gifts God loves to see us use for Him.

Marissa: So God likes it when I sing?

Mom: Of course. He gave it to you. He likes to hear you sing even more than I do. And you know I do! We give to God when we use our gifts for Him.

Marissa: Cool!

Mom: Marissa, I want to teach you a little poem to remember, anytime you wonder who gave you all the gifts that make you special.

Marissa: OK!

Mom: Here goes:
   Who gave me the talents I bring
   The songs that I sing
   God gave it to me
   He gave me the gifts that I give
   The life that I live
   He gave it to me!

Marissa: I can do that!
   Who gave me the talents I bring
   The songs that I sing
   God gave it to me
   He gave me the gifts that I give
   The life that I live
   He gave it to me!

[Both exit. Begin music.]

Announcer: *[Offstage]* Who gave you the gifts that you have? God did. He's blessed you with many special abilities. You can use them to give glory back to God. Use your gifts for God!

[Fade music.]